Invisible
Influence

Invisible
Influence

The Power to Persuade
Anyone, Anytime, Anywhere

Kevin Hogan

WILEY

Cover design: Susan Olinsky

Published by John Wiley & Sons, Inc., Hoboken, New Jersey.
Published simultaneously in Canada.

For general information about our other products and services, please contact our Customer Care
Department within the United States at (800) 762-2974, outside the United States at (317) 572-3993
or fax (317) 572-4002.

Wiley publishes in a variety of print and electronic formats and by print-on-demand. Some material
included with standard print versions of this book may not be included in e-books or in print-on-
demand. If this book refers to media such as a CD or DVD that is not included in the version you
purchased, you may download this material at http://booksupport.wiley.com. For more information
about Wiley products, visit www.wiley.com.

Library of Congress Cataloging-in-Publication Data:
Hogan, Kevin.
    Invisible influence: the power to persuade anyone, anytime, anywhere/Kevin Hogan.
        pages cm
    Includes bibliographical references.
    ISBN 978-1-118-60225-6 (hbk. : alk. paper); ISBN 978-1-118-62047-2 (ebk);
ISBN 978-1-118-62046-5 (ebk): ISBN 978-1-118-62039-7 (ebk)
    1. Persuasion (Psychology) 2. Influence (Psychology) 3. Interpersonal communication. I.
Title.
    HM1196. H64 2013
    303.3'42—dc23
                                                                                    2012048008
Printed in the United States of America.

10 9 8 7 6 5 4 3 2 1

For Mark, Jessica, and Katie

Contents

Acknowledgments

I want to thank Mark Hogan for making this book better. Every day for an hour he'd take me away from writing to play catch, chess, or Rockband. Those breaks helped me return to the manuscript and instantly find a dozen ways to make something better for you, the reader. More than anything, the nightly hug from a 15-year-old young man and "I love you, Dad" drives me to be the best I can be. I have the greatest son in the world.

Thanks to Katie Hogan for tolerating me while under the influence of yet another book being written. There is a real tension between author and the rest of the world that exists when a manuscript is being penned. It must be tougher to navigate through and around that tension than I often estimate in real time. There are plenty of bonus challenges each day when the person you live with is an author. I'm well aware that I'm not all that charismatic when I'm researching, not so charming during rewrites, and not even close to tolerable during editing. I love you.

Jessica Hogan continues to inspire me as she works toward her PsyD down in Chicago. Just knowing she's down there keeps my competitive edge "on." I no longer feel like she's in "my world." I now feel like I'm in hers. Taking on grad school with the handicap of profound hearing loss makes me doubly proud of her tenacity. I don't know how she could be in class, do labs, and work with children, all while hearing only some of the words being spoken. She could moan about her disability and no one would think less of her. Instead she works damned hard and carries on without complaint. I couldn't be prouder. She's an inspiration to everyone around her.

I want to thank my editor Rachel Hastings for pushing me to continually make this book better for you. She had the audacity to regularly suggest that "You talked about something like that in *Science of Influence*. Do you really want that in this book?" My favorite is when she says, "This technique is weak. I saw something like this in so-and-so's book. I'm taking it out." She wasn't going to let anything slide. Her constant suggestions and sometimes sweeping changes were not only annoying, they were absolutely necessary in bringing you what is in your hands.

Jim Speakman, my co-author of *Covert Persuasion,* was a true creative impetus behind this project. He encouraged me to do an influence book, including techniques I hadn't previously written about. After we wrote *Covert Persuasion,* which was loaded with "tactics" and "techniques," it seemed like everyone came out with a technique book of their own. If imitation is the best form of flattery, then we were very flattered. Mackenzie and Madison (Jim's kids) seem to play a role in all of Jim's ideas.

The members of my Platinum Inner Circle, without question, are the daily force that drives me to not just keep up but get ahead of the curve. They are Duane Cunningham, Clare Delaney, Annie Born, Lisa Hyatt, Octavio Urzua, Todd Gaster, Scott Bell, Dale Bell, Christian Haller, Bryan Lenihan, Sonya Lenzo, April Braswell, Rob Northrup, Steve Chambers, Ken Owens, Michael Walker, Cherie Miranda, and Larry Hines.

I want to thank Roberto Monaco of www.influenceology.com for letting me use his story in the Technique section.

Bob Beverley has had a greater impact on me than he knows. Now he knows. Special thanks to David Garfinkel and Deb Cole.

Thanks to Andrew Records for making www.KevinHoganUniversity .com a great place for our team to work.

Special thanks to Gary Moon and Wendy Schauer for always having something good to say when the rest of the world said something else.

Thanks to all the great researchers around the world from whom I drew ideas or quotes from their press releases or studies. They are the heroes of persuasion and influence.

Thanks to Matt Holt, Shannon Vargo, Tiffany Colon, and Linda Indig at Wiley. They are a pleasure to work with and made this a better book!

1

Intentional Reality

You're about to meet someone and the stakes are high.

You're about to ask them a question that really matters. Perhaps the answer will determine your income, your job security, whether you'll have the date with the cute girl next week . . . or not.

But I have bad news.

They are going to say no.

You can change that right now, if you can wrap your mind around the fact that the birthplace of influence is in your own brain.

What the person is going to be like, and what their response to you and your request is going to be is, in significant part, happening right now between your ears.

In His Own Image

The Bible says that God created man in "his own image."

It turns out that God gave man a touch of that creative power as well.

This story about how you shape others in your own image has a few twists and turns, and a surprise ending with a lot of *Aha*s and *Wows* in between. You may never see yourself or others in the same way.

The truth is that yes and no often rest squarely on the *creative power of your imagination*.

Let me explain that. Go back with me to a time in the not-so-distant past. We're at the University of Minnesota, in 1977.[1]

---

[1] M. Snyder, E. Tanke, and E. Berscheid, "Social Perception and Interpersonal Behavior: On the Self-Fulfilling Nature of Social Stereotypes," *Journal of Personality and Social Psychology* 35, no. 9 (September 1977): 656–666.

Fifty-one men and women are paired up to have a telephone conversation. They are told they are part of a nonverbal communication study that looks at the process of how people become acquainted when they do not meet in person, and there are no nonverbal elements present.

The women in each pair fill out a brief background profile, giving information about their schooling, education, and other facts that we know to be totally irrelevant to how people actually get acquainted.

The man has his photo taken and is given the information sheet, along with a photo of a woman. The photo he receives is one of a selection of four photos of women whose average attractiveness is rated as 8.1 (on a scale of 1 to 10) or a photo of one of four women whose average attractiveness is 2.56. The photo is *not* of the woman he can't see in the other room. She has no idea he has been given a supposed picture of her.

Armed with only this information, the men record their impressions of the women before the call.

After a 10-minute conversation the man completes another impression sheet on the woman. She, in turn, provides information on how comfortable she was with the conversation, how accurate a picture of herself her partner had formed, and how typical her partner was in terms of his treatment of her. Finally she records her prediction of what the man rated her personal attractiveness to be.

Later, 12 people listen to an audio, which only contains the woman's side of the conversation. Based only on this, they provide an assessment of her looks and personality. Nine other judges listen to a recording of just the man's side of the conversation and give their impressions of him.

None of these observer judges are given a photo or any other information.

What were the results?

1. The men's initial impressions, after seeing the photo but prior to the conversation, showed that the photo biased his overall impression of the woman. When shown a photo of an attractive woman, the men anticipated her to be more social, poised, humorous, and socially adept. When shown the photo of the unattractive woman, the men's perceptions of her were typically as unsocial, awkward, serious, and socially inept. In total, men assigned 17 of 21 personality traits the researchers predicted would be attributed to the attractive women based on her photo.

You already might have guessed that. But here's the really interesting part.

2. The observer judges *also* assigned the same traits to the women that the men did, solely on the basis of listening to the woman's side of the recorded call. Remember, they had never seen a photo!

If a man had seen a photo of an attractive woman and ascribed positive personality traits to her, then the judges recorded the same perception of that woman based solely on *listening* to her side of the conversation.

If a man had seen a photo of one of the unattractive women, the judges ascribed very different personality characteristics to that woman based on only her four minutes of recorded conversation. And remember, there were 51 pairs!

The researchers (Mark Snyder, Elizabeth Tanke, and Ellen Berscheid) concluded, after a thorough statistical analysis, that, "What had initially been reality in the minds of the men, had become reality in the behavior of the women they interacted with—a discernible reality by even naive observer judges, who had access to only . . . recordings of the women's contributions to the conversations."

And what about the men? How did the judges rate their personality traits?

Based on only the men's side of the conversation, the group of judges who had not heard the women or known about any photos had the following perceptions: if the man was looking at the photo of an attractive woman *he* was ascribed traits of higher physical attraction, more confidence, and more animation than the men who were looking at a photo of an unattractive woman. In addition, those who had seen the photo of the attractive woman were *themselves* seen as taking greater initiative, being more comfortable, and enjoying themselves more. Finally, the observers believed that the "attractive" women would see the man as attractive, in contrast to those men who had seen the photo of the unattractive woman.

The "attractive" target women (whether they were or were not attractive we will never know) believed their partner saw them more accurately, and the unattractive target women believed their partner did not. The researchers suggest that may be why the results were achieved.

The implications are mind-blowing.

What can you do with this information?

If you are male, what would happen if you had a picture of an attractive woman in view as you worked on the telephone setting appointments, consummating the business deal, or communicating with a woman for any reason? It would seem likely that more appointments would be set, more deals would be sealed, and communication would be vastly improved.

And what about women who communicate predominantly with men? Would the same strategy be effective? It has not been tested, but my guess is that it would.

Maybe it would even work at creating better outcomes with the same gender.

The study clearly shows how much we are influenced by people's appearance.

But more importantly, doesn't the research imply that our biases change people's behaviors?

That's exactly what it implies.

The notion that a belief that has been held for one minute about the attractiveness of the woman you are speaking with, and the impact on how you are *both* perceived by people listening in, is remarkable.

The lessons here are many:

- Attractive people are ascribed positive personality and social traits that unattractive people are not.
- One person's reality is communicated vocally in such a way that a belief held for one minute can transform another person into who they are perceived to be by the person they are in conversation with.
- Believing you are interacting with someone attractive changes you: your self-perception, your behavior, your attitudes. And the opposite is true as well.
- Your certainties about someone will impact them.

Now let's look at the "Prophecy Effect."

Does what you think *really* shape others?

Every day you might typically run into 100 people. Each of those people sees you in some distinct way. So, do they *all* shape your behavior? And if so, wouldn't that create you and me in the image of how society as a whole sees us?

The Powerful Influence of Prophecy

Two psychologists visit a 15-week military boot camp for experienced soldiers in Israel.[2] They want to know what a commanding officer's beliefs and expectations will do to those he trains.

One hundred and five soldiers are assigned one of three labels by the psychologists visiting Boot Camp. The psychologists meet with the base commander and the four commanders doing the training. The base commander is the only person let in on the secret.

The psychologists explain that they have developed a complex method to predict the Command Potential of the 105 trainees. They show the four instructors their results and ask them to record this prediction of Command Potential in the files of the 105 recruits. The predictions include one of three words:

- High
- Regular
- Unknown

Over the course of 15 weeks of advanced training, the long-time soldiers are to be evaluated by their own instructors, as well as external assessors, based on their theoretical knowledge of combat tactics, topography, standard operating procedures, and practical skills of navigation and firing a weapon. Their Combat Potential has been randomly assigned.

One week into training, the commanders rank the Command Potential (CP) of the trainees.

After one week, the influence of the CP the commanders received from the psychologists on the 1–9 ratings they recorded is already significant:

- 6.83 average scores are given to those randomly assigned with High CP.
- 5.31 average scores are given to those randomly assigned with Unknown CP.
- 4.32 average scores are given to those randomly assigned with Regular CP.

Because of the dramatic results, the psychologists take several precautions with the base commander to ensure all trainees are treated well and that their future career will not be negatively impacted as a result of the study.

---

[2] D. Eden and A. Shani, "Pygmalion Goes to Boot Camp: Expectancy, Leadership, and Trainee Performance," *Journal of Applied Psychology* 67, no. 2 (April 1982): 194–199.

At the end of the 15 weeks, the soldiers are assessed by independent military trainers. The scores for trainee performance are as follows:

- 79.98 average scores are given to those randomly assigned with High CP.
- 72.43 average scores are given to those randomly assigned with Unknown CP.
- 65.18 average scores are given to those randomly assigned with Regular CP.

Stunning and dramatic differences, right?

The researchers' (Dov Eden and Abraham Shani) findings were mind-boggling.

It was evident that a commander's beliefs would change and shape the performance of even experienced men, with an average of 11 years each in the military. More remarkably, once debriefed, the experienced instructors on base didn't believe the results and didn't believe the fact that the men had been randomly assigned CP by the psychologists.

The power of *real* expectation is to be taken seriously.

These two studies highlight the fact that no one was doing "affirmations," like "I *think* I can," or *trying* to manipulate behavior. These people were **convinced** about the truths they were dealing with.

Statistical analysis showed that 73 percent of the variance in the results on performance came down to Instructor Expectancy.

If you move that expectancy into a classroom, then the difference between a child getting a "B" and "D" *could* mostly be generated from the teacher.

Thinking positively, or negatively, about someone isn't going to cut it in the real world. In fact, it could easily have the opposite effect. However, one piece of compelling evidence that causes us to have **certainty** about another, something as simple as an errant photo or a word transcribed from a psychologist's notes to a military file folder, can change someone's perceived personality, their performance, and ultimately where they end up in life.

One word. One photo.

I can almost hear you saying, "Okay, that *is* amazing, but *how* do I make that happen in my life with the girl, with the client, with the kids, with the spouse, with the neighbor?"

Let me share with you what I refer to in my work as The Expectant Mind.

The Expectant Mind allows you to change your Self and Others.

Everyone has an Expectant Mind. Our beliefs, attitudes, values, nonconscious attention, nonconscious goal pursuit are all frozen in concrete.

Fundamental beliefs (in every sense of the word) about self and beliefs about others are not only sticky. They are solid.

A tiny percentage of people have the current skill set to shift their current Expectant Mind and deliberately craft it into a Mind that can change themselves and others in a unique and powerful way.

How many people have the capacity to shift to the Expectant Mind that causes them to have what they want?

Most.

How many people know *how* to do it?

Just a few.

How many will do it if you give them the formula?

You tell me.

What the Expectant Mind Is Not

- You didn't convince yourself of something.
- You can't recite affirmations and come to believe something that you are not certain of.
- It isn't stating something to yourself or to a group that you aren't absolutely certain of, and believing change will magically happen.

The Expectant Mind is absolutely convinced of the truth of some belief, notion, or idea to the point where it *is simply not questioned.* There is no reason for the conscious mind to doubt the fact and bring the notion to awareness.

Examples:

- You look and say, "That's the sun." And it is.
- You look and say, "That's where I work." And you do.
- You say, "That's my car." It is.

In each case, you could be hallucinating. You could be wrong and think it's your car but actually it's someone else's car.

How is the certainty of reality significant in the studies we just looked at?

The Expectant Mind **knew** that he was looking at a photo of the woman he was talking to on the phone, even though it was simply a photo of a woman at the University. The Expectant Mind of the military instructor "knew" that certain trainees were going to have high Command Potential.

They had no reason to question the facts, even though they weren't facts at all. They were simply pieces of information that were not critically analyzed by the individual. They became more than beliefs. They became "the sun," "my car."

The Expectant Mind is beyond certain. It's not arrogant. That would mean The Mind is correct or right about something. The Expectant Mind is not *right*. It is not *wrong*. It simply has accepted inputs as facts and leaves the facts and moves on.

There is no wondering.

There is no investigation.

That's pretty profound stuff. . . .

The question is, how do you generate an Expectant Mind so that you make more sales, get more yeses, and achieve change in others, a mind where you have absolute fact expectations (the sun will rise in the morning) without having the trait of arrogance and other instant turn-offs?

Step back and ponder this.

People have evolved to use each other as mirrors. You ask someone how you look because without a mirror you don't know. You tend to mirror other people's behavior because of mirror neurons in your brain, so long as there are no internal triggers *not* to mirror another's behavior. The mirroring effect is an absolutely crucial element in changing yourself and others because **their brain literally sees and hears your certainty**.

Their brain replicates those inputs without any conscious processing at all, and it becomes certain that *you* know what you're talking about. Without having any kind of psychic or paranormal powers, your nonverbal or inner truth is authentically readable to the other on a very deep biological level.

The women in the study didn't *think* about how they behaved on the phone. **The men didn't *try* to change either their behavior or that**

of the women. The men changed who the women "were" because of *how* they communicated with them, and how those inputs were received and processed.

The soldiers in the study didn't end up shooting better, navigating better or showing evidence of greater command potential because they "thought about it." **The trainers didn't "try" to get the soldiers to behave in some new way.** The trainers had no idea how their communication was affecting each person. It simply did because the commanders were primed. They were convinced, to the point of not thinking about it, that certain soldiers had higher Command Potential than others.

Now Expectancy grows clearer.

How do you **cause** the girl to admire you?

How do you **cause** the soldier to achieve to his peak potential?

How do you **cause** the employee to perform?

How do you **cause** the prospect to say yes?

How do you **cause** people to change their behavior?

You've learned it has nothing to do with bogus affirmations. There is no connection here with "positive thinking."

So, how do you create an Expectant Mind that will enable certainty to be replicated in the mind of another when you communicate with them?

Certain about themselves.

Certain about you.

Here's the thing: Would you agree that most people are intimidated by actually thinking something through?

They want a script to get the girl.

They want a script to give the telemarketer.

They want a script to sell a product online.

They want words given to them such that when they say them, they will magically change someone. That works at Hogwarts. It doesn't work in real life. The funniest thing in the world is watching people sell something and say, "Here's the script, just do this and you'll get this result."

People want to believe that if they copy something that worked for someone else it will work for them, too.

Then the individual will spend $2,000 on a turnkey wealth-building or success system and find out that it doesn't work. They are surprised, shocked, depressed. Why? They truly believed that it was in the "exact words," the exact marketing script, hypnosis script, sales script . . . they are all the same. Ultimately they don't work beyond slightly more than chance. Scripts work in a play where actors practice and rehearse how they interact with others and the story and the audience. In situations where all actors are not rehearsing an agreed script, the script essentially will fail.

Save your money.

The exact words have very little to do with getting someone to say yes. There are exceptions. I've written about such exceptions, but an Expectant Mind is the sun coming up in the morning, compared to lighting a match in a dark corner.

The men in the study didn't intentionally say *anything* to change the behavior of the women. It was their certainty (and errant belief) in her image that created the effect. That photo *first* triggered behaviors in the man, which changed his attitudes, his behavior, then her self-concept, her behavior, and finally the beliefs of independent people listening to audiotapes weeks later.

The Expectant Mind.

The layers are starting to peel away.

You are starting to see what doesn't work.

You can't wish for it.

You can't pray for it.

You can't hope for it.

You can't generate it from willpower.

You can't force it to happen.

You can't say words to yourself and make something up.

What you need to do is to optimize your mind to the point where you have an Expectant Mind that is deliberately *different* from what it is today.

The best predictor of over 90 percent of people's life situations in five years' time is to look at what they are doing today. Most of them won't change themselves, they won't evolve, and they can't change others. They want exact words and they don't want to *understand* how and what is happening in a conversation, in a picture, in a video. They want the beautiful model handed to them on the plate without working for her.

She's not coming.

*Exact words are only effective when matched with outputs that will trigger mirror neurons to tell **their brain** that (1) you are 100 percent correct and (2) that they believe you without question.*

I assume you want the girl or guy to say yes.

I assume you want to make more money, have a more successful business.

I assume you want to change people, to influence people.

I assume you want to be a trigger of change.

In almost all cases, wherever your life is heading is very close to where it will end up.

If you don't change, they don't change. You always get what you have now and move further in that direction whatever it is to the ultimate end goal of bankruptcy, foreclosure, default, and failure.

When you are certain in your communication beyond question, they agree. Period. If you aren't a credible source, you fail. If you are **source credible**, you will succeed.

That's *not* the same as a date. That's the same as the 9.7 model having one drink with your 7.0 self. The date comes next.

The date can only happen, the big sale can only happen *if* the certainty in your mind triggers the mirror neurons in their mind.

Women will tell you there are two kinds of guys that approach them with similar characteristics. They both approach, ask, expect yes, and have pure confidence. The women only say yes (to some things) when the guy meets a high enough score on her Guyometer.

The same is true with a sales call. The same is true with marketing. It's all the same.

It begins with your absolute certainty they will behave in a certain manner. You wouldn't think of trying to cause the behavior. Your communication is merely a function of your **identity**. You don't *try* to do anything. This is just how you now are.

By causing a person to behave in a way they normally wouldn't, you create cognitive dissonance. That means they have two conflicting values, attitudes, actions, or beliefs going on in their brain at the same time. They don't like that. They need to fix it.

The girl is having a drink with you and you have seconds to make a convert. If your perception is that girls like this always say no, then you have 0 percent chance of yes. If your perception is that girls like this have said no in the past it is *because of some reason*, which you can truly understand. You can turn that into something different as you go forward. You have reframed the picture. **You are no longer the same person.** You have gone from a certain no to a likely yes where you would be surprised, no, stunned at no.

You do *not* need to figure out why you are so amazing because you probably aren't and, if you were, the last thing you want to do is reinforce that by fine-tuning the fact.

You need to figure out why *all* those people said no in the past. You need to dissociate from the picture, see yourself in the picture, and describe in massive detail why things happened in the past as they did. You don't have to make anything up and if you do you simply fail more as time goes on.

All you want to do is write about *why they said no*. And write a lot. The girl? The marketing sales letter? The sales call? It's literally all the same thing. It's someone saying no to you who you would have wanted to say yes.

Think back to the research. The women behaved differently from each other because of the photo the guy held. His confidence and certainty sold her one way or the other. The trainers in Israel? They simply *knew* the recruits they were assigned with high Command Potential would do well, then didn't think about it again. They just . . . knew. They were certain. They didn't think about it. It wasn't even a given. It just *was*.

Developing Your New Expectant Mind

Your brain is a storytelling machine.

It only learns through fluid concepts and story. That's it.

A lengthy, detailed, completely plausible, reality-based story *will* generate a result very different than your current story, unless of course your current story is getting you precisely what you want, instead of what you don't want.

Here's the Template

1. Take a half-hour every day for one week and use your camera or DVR or pen and paper and record why all those things happened in the past. Go into a half-hour of detail. Writing is probably best, but video or audio could do the trick if you are a well organized thinker.
2. Next week turn your attention to the future. Using great detail, create a complete movie or screenplay for your future. Not 2050 but 2017. Go

into massive detail, using lots of sequences to show what leads to what, why things happen, and your response and reactions to what happens each day and hour. No hype. Your brain *must* buy into your story 100 percent. It *must* be 100 percent plausible or you might as well go to the beach and get a tan.

3. If you want to **change them** you must **reframe them**. You must go back in your mind and find out why all that happened with those significant people before you met them. Describe it all in massive detail, like a movie where everything is fully fleshed out and you understand everything. But you aren't making stuff up; it's real. It *has* to be real. Then turn to the future and how future similar experiences will turn out (sales calls, getting the girl to say yes, positive reaction to your sales letters, people admiring you, and so on and so forth).

Be meticulous and thorough in your use of detail. Take one week. Do this each day. Write five pages of text both for the past and the future.

If you don't do this, you are simply 100 percent normal and you will, with absolute certainty, get the exact same results you always have gotten. This is simply your choice to completely rewrite the script that has passed, and to write a desirable, plausible screenplay for the future.

If you **do** do this, you will become expectant.

You will develop a nonarrogant self-certainty that will probably drive some people nuts simply because they will never get what they want out of life, but **you** will.

It's simple science. It's work, and because of that you will never be the same and people will never respond to you in the same way again.

And yes, it really is all the same. It's not the words. You'll succeed at most things involving people and hear yes when you ask, far more often than you will hear no. You'll start to see that people respond to you almost identically in all contexts as you reshape who you are by reframing your past and creating the screenplay for your future.

Performance of any kind requires more preparation than meets the eye. Every top performer in sports absolutely knows that once they hit the playing field they will win, even when they ultimately lose.

Invisible Influence begins with an Expectant Mind and it stops without it.

2 | Identity Convergence

You may or may not know your Self, but you're about to see how those you influence will identify with you to the point they will do burdensome tasks they normally wouldn't do for you, just because you asked.

Two female undergraduates sit across from each other doing a task, crossing out letters *L*, *K*, and *S* on a puzzle sheet.[1] One is in on the experiment and known as a "confederate." The experimenter leaves the room after they begin. The timer goes off. Two minutes pass. The experimenter returns.

There are three conditions in this experiment:

1. The confederate briefly converses with the other woman after the task, before the experimenter returns.
2. The confederate and the other woman sit silently until the experimenter returns.
3. A woman does the puzzle alone.

The experimenter collects puzzle sheets and gives credit toward graduation in all three conditions.

In each condition the women leave the room. Once outside the confederate pulls an essay from her backpack and asks a "huge favor" of the other woman.

---

[1] J.M. Burger, S. Soroka, K. Gonzago, E. Murphy, and E. Somervel, "The Effect of Fleeting Attraction on Compliance to Requests," *Personality and Social Psychology Bulletin* 27, no. 12 (December 2001): 1578–1586.

"I have an eight-page paper that I need someone I don't know to read and write a one-page paper with written comments as to whether it was persuasive or not. Would you do it?"

Here's what happens, related to the three conditions of the experiment:

1. 48.7 percent agree.
2. 48.6 percent agree.
3. 26.3 percent agree.

The two women in conditions **1** and **2** have shared an experience. They identify with each other.

In a later study the conditions were manipulated a little differently to test if the willingness to help extended to "strangers." Here's what happened:

1. The women sit silently together and a different confederate asks the favor of the subject: 22.5 percent agree to help.
2. Women sit silently together and the confederate who shared the experience asks the favor: 55 percent agree to help.
3. A woman sits by herself and does the puzzle piece and is approached when she leaves: 20 percent agree to help.

The woman isn't going to help an *unknown* person with the eight-page task, but she is willing to help the confederate she has been through a shared experience with, in more than half the cases.

In another study, a similar experiment was carried out with about 100 women.

The experimenter says to each woman he meets with individually in the room, "You and someone else will learn about each other."

The experimenter gives the woman a list of 50 adjectives to choose from and tells her to "circle 20 that describe yourself."

After completion, the experimenter takes the list, leaves, and eventually returns to the woman with the adjective list that her "partner next door" has filled out. This is not true; it is a dummy sheet. He hands the partner's list to the woman and presents one of the following options:

1. 3 out of 20 traits match between the woman and the confederate.
2. 10 out of 20 traits match between the woman and the confederate.
3. 17 out of 20 traits match between the woman and the confederate.

The confederate and the woman are brought together to meet. Then, the confederate asks the woman to read and critique the eight-page essay:

1. 43.3 percent of those in the 3 out of 20 group agree to help.
2. 60 percent of those in the 10 out of 20 group agree to help.
3. 76.7 percent of those in the 17 out of 20 group agree to help.

The more characteristics the women believe that they and the unseen confederate have in common, the more likely they are to agree to help with the one-hour task.

In a follow-up study an experimenter tested the significance of women sharing the same birthday in the puzzle task.

What happened?

When the woman discovered the confederate shared the same birthday, she complied with the request from the confederate 62.2 percent of the time.

When she was told a birthday that was not her own, she complied 34.2 percent of the time.

Simply mentioning the word "birthday" triggered significantly more compliance than the 20 to 25 percent we've come to expect in the experiment.

In another related experiment, when the woman was told that she and the confederate shared the same type of common fingerprints, she complied with the request from the confederate 54.8 percent of the time. When she was told they shared a rare fingerprint type, the woman complied 82.1 percent of the time![2]

When people spend even a few minutes together, they are significantly more likely to take on a burdensome task when asked.

When people believe they have something in common with others, they are significantly more likely to take on a burdensome task when asked.

When people believe they have something rare in common with another, they are *dramatically* more likely to take on a burdensome task when asked.

Identification leads to Trust, which leads to Reduced Resistance, which leads to Compliance.

Let's examine this from the standpoint of identity.

---

[2] J.M. Burger, N. Messian, S. Patel, A. del Prado, and C. Anderson, "What a Coincidence! The Effects of Incidental Similarity on Compliance," *Personality and Social Psychology Bulletin* 30, no. 1 (January 2004): 35–43.

Your Identity begins with The Group, the collective. You are part of The Group. You will do a great deal to ensure the continuance and success of The Group.

When you were born you were cared for by a select number of people. Perhaps Mother, or Mother and Father, or Father and Nanny, or something along those lines. Your world consisted of you, five faces you saw every day, plus a dog or cat against the outside world.

That was your first group. Attachment (or love) was generated within a specific context. You imprinted on these people. That is to say, the faces that looked at you became an integral part of your Self-Identity. Your parent was as much a part of you as anyone else ever would be in life.

You adopted their behaviors, their attitudes, their feelings, their thoughts.

You went to their favorite restaurant, drank their favorite soft drink, and ate their favorite meals. Those experiences generally "stuck" to become a part of you.

Your identity was made up of "You, plus those in your home" (Mom, Dad, siblings, the babysitter) versus Everyone Else.

It was the first We versus Them in your world.

Then you found neighbors. They became a lesser We, but a We nonetheless. If something negatively affected the neighbors, it most probably did the same to your family. The shared experiences of neighbors (the weather, crime, and so on) bind them together to make a We. But this We is also part of Them, the larger, bigger world. All things being equal, you'll trust and believe your neighbor but not to the degree you'd believe part of your We inside the home.

Your We became bigger as you gained mobility, went shopping with your parents, met other kids in the neighborhood, went to school, went to church. Generally, school is the greatest single Time Influence on behavior, and school becomes a big part of the We and They equation. You might be a Gopher or a Buckeye, but you certainly don't consider everyone at school your friend or trusted ally. Even though you are a Gopher, there are parts of that identity that are threatened and inconsistent because of the bullies, jerks, and so on.

As you become part of more groups and make greater personal investment, you develop multiple identities and your behavior changes from group to group, from environment to environment. You'll behave differently in England than you do in the United States. You need a lot more help when you are outside of your own environment. You are on *their* turf and that is *not* a part of your identity. You will do whatever it takes to survive their turf and return to your own. In simple terms, you're a lot more likely to be friendly with strangers in other countries than you are in your own country.

The more different Their country is from your country, the more your behavior will change to what you perceive to be the smartest, safest, and wisest set of actions you can take in any given moment.

Fairly early in life, your identity in its most base form is your physical body and how it compares and contrasts to the group. "I am skinny." "I am fat." "I am nearsighted." "I am hard of hearing." These are all Identities or Identity Elements, and they determine your behaviors along with the external experiences with The Group and The Out Group.

Your identity is also your ability to manipulate whatever intelligences, personality traits, mental functions and dysfunctions, and traits you possess and how your mental agility compares and contrasts to the group.

Your identity (or an identity) can encompass your position and significance in the group in various roles.

Your identity is individualized or collectivized based upon how the group views all of the parts of the bigger whole.

Your identity is the role you play as a productive or nonproductive human. You might be a salesperson or a manager. You could be an author.

Your identity changes as you move from context to context. You might be a pastor at church on Sunday but a humble janitor Monday through Friday.

Your identity changes as you move from group to group. You might be known as someone of great status and dominance in your group, but have no status or dominance when you enter the auto mechanic's shop.

You have more than one identity. Being a spouse and being a parent are generally two very different identities. Being a parent and being a manager might seem to be the same identity, but they aren't. You can't fire your children and rarely do they quit.

If you want to be like everyone in The Group, you will adopt their behavioral choices. If you want to be different from everyone in The Group, you will repel their behavioral choices. If you want to be considered part of The Group but not an "assimilated Borg," you'll support the group but find safe differences.

And remember there are a number of Groups in your life.

There is a knock on the door. One of your Groups is the person or people who live inside of the house or apartment. Everyone outside is typically experienced as part of They, so the unexpected knock on the door is not generally felt with joy. Perhaps the knock triggers anxiety or urgency. For some it triggers boredom or a sense of familiarity if the door was knocked on regularly when one was young.

The unexpected knock on the door is a signal of a potential intruder. (So are the sounds of windows opening that aren't supposed to be opening.)

When you don't recognize the person at the door, *and* they are not generally attractive to you, you will feel something that could range from a sense of discomfort to outright fear.

They are knocking on the door because they *want something* from you. You know this as you open the door. That means you experience resistance before you even grab the doorknob.

When the door opens if you pleasantly recognize the person, you feel a sense of relief and release.

Perhaps a welcome visitor!

But if you don't recognize them, the resistance grows bigger. The only factor that might defuse that sensation would be a very attractive face at the door, which would feed the brain's reward centers, offsetting or eliminating most of the resistance you feel. In the more common case where you have the person who wants something without your reward center being lit up, you have a challenge. You might wish to be kind and considerate to this person, but your brain has set off alarms causing a burst of adrenaline to protect you just in case.

You can change how people feel, think, and behave through the simplest of influences, creating subtle threads of identification that most people would never notice.

Not long ago, some brilliantly conceived experiments revealed just how powerful Invisible Influence is.

Why is it that some (but not all) women at the mall feel more glamorous, good looking, and feminine simply by toting around a Victoria's Secret bag instead of a similar pink shopping bag?

They weren't using a product. They were simply carrying around an empty shopping bag.

Women who carried around a pink bag reported nothing out of the ordinary.

The Victoria's Secret bag, however, had magic in it.

But the magic of Invisible Influence is not necessarily intuitive influence. Most marketers, salespeople, and advertisers guess. They follow their intuition and hope it leads them to the right answer. And that strategy doesn't work very well. . . .

Minnesota researchers found that a single specific type of woman reported feeling more glamorous and even better looking after an hour with the VS bag in contrast to a similar generic pink bag.[3]

Women who believe that their personality is not fixed but can change are *not* influenced by carrying the VS bag. They report no impact from carrying the bag.

However, those who believe that they are not able to change themselves (in other words, they are who they are) feel more glamorous and attractive when carrying the bag.

The **VS** bag versus a generic pink bag causes the "*fixed mindset woman*" to feel sexier because the bag acts as a trigger to her nonconscious and as a signal to the general public. "I am like a VS girl, not because I have become sexier, but because the bag has imbued me with something I didn't possess."

The bag has rubbed off its magical power on women who "know" they aren't going to change.

The first crucial point here of course is that what is intuitive is often not correct. The Victoria's Secret bag causes some women to feel sexier. Others feel no change.

The same researchers went on to test the power of the influence of brand characteristics on another group of people. I'll lay that out for you in a moment.

You, yourself, are a brand. People who know you have come to ascribe specific traits to you. Companies often are well branded in such a way that the general public perceives the company's brand to embody a specific set of traits.

I think of Apple computers as a creative, superior, and intelligent brand.

---

[3] Ji Kyung Park and Deborah Roedder John, "Got to Get You into My Life: Do Brand Personalities Rub Off on Consumers?" *Journal of Consumer Research*, 37, no. 4 (December 2010): 655–669.

You could speculate that people who do not believe that they can change their personality or intelligence might benefit greatly from using a computer that is branded as creative, superior, and intelligent—and you might be right.

Giving hundreds of people an Apple computer to use in an experiment is rather difficult, so a simpler form of influence was introduced to a group of MBA students at the University of Minnesota.

An M.I.T. pen.

M.I.T. sounds like something you catch a baseball with if you aren't a graduate student at the university. But at the university you know that M.I.T. stands for hardworking intelligent leaders. That is the M.I.T. brand. And students were given a pen with the M.I.T. logo to use for six weeks.

What happened at the end of the six weeks?

For those students who believed they can change and that they have flexible intelligence capabilities?

Nothing.

For those students who believed they are who they are and they aren't ever going to change?

They believed themselves to be more hardworking, more of a leader, and more intelligent.

Then the researchers constructed a brilliant experiment where students were either given an article about how people can change or an article about how they don't change. They then were given either a Victoria's Secret shopping bag or a pink bag for a treasure hunt at the university.

Those students who had read the article saying people don't change, and then went on to collect items in the Victoria's Secret bag, reported that they were more glamorous, good-looking, and feminine.

Those who read the article noting that people can change?

It didn't matter whether they carried a Victoria's Secret bag or not. There was no magic in either bag.

People who don't believe they can change are likely to be strongly attracted to brands because of the desirable attributes the brand signals to the individual and also to those who see the individual using the brand.

Meanwhile, people who believe they can change certainly might purchase branded products, but the magic of the brand to enhance self-perception of the key traits of the brand simply doesn't "work" on those who know they are able to improve the self.

I recently asked myself, "When do I use brands to impress or signal to others?"

Unless I'm traveling, I rarely go out to eat, so I experience no interest in signaling in that area.

I collect jewelry owned by Elvis Presley, autographs of well-known celebrities, but I don't wear the rings or necklaces I collect. No one sees them except me. (That is kind of ridiculous now that I ponder it.)

I drive a vehicle that I purchased during 2010 when there was a tax break for buying a vehicle greater than 6,000 pounds. I never would have bought an SUV to save my soul . . . but to get the tax break? I'm a proud owner of a Toyota Sequoia.

Up until last month when I received a new piece of luggage for my birthday, I traveled with a beat-up suitcase that had been around the world with me. I wear old Levi Jeans. Not Lucky's, as I've been encouraged to do.

I don't have any fancy pens that I use. I tend to have a pad of paper and prefer it for notetaking over a computer or similar.

I was finding myself ridiculously improvement-oriented until it hit me. I like to wear my Hugo Boss jacket when I fly because I don't want the flight attendant to see the label that says Target (or whatever it says, I don't know because I don't want anyone to see it!).

There it is.

The inside of that jacket, which goes immediately into the jacket hold upon boarding, is seen *only* by the flight attendant who takes my coat and retrieves it at the end of the flight. That one woman. That's it. I have no idea when I leave town if she will be beautiful or plain, but my nonconscious mind is telling me to signal to her that I am fashionably savvy.

And now that I think about it, I am self-conscious about it. I really don't want the woman to see Made in Indonesia or whatever I would prefer to wear onto the plane.

Go figure. Something buried deep within me felt compelled to signal status and prestige to a flight attendant.

Not to my doctor, a nurse, a therapist, an audience, a maid, a house-keeper, a hotel front desk employee, my neighbors. There must be *someone* else out there in the world I'm trying to signal, and I'll let you know, but between now and then, just know that my nonconscious mind must have something plotted for a flight attendant. I'll keep you posted. . . .

I am influenced by what the flight attendant might think of me. That's an invisible influence. I never really thought about it until now.

Most people have numerous brands from which they receive magic, the transference of specific brand traits from the brand to the person, because they believe themselves unchangeable at least in certain ways.

In other words, if I want to appear and feel *more creative*, I should bring the Mac with me on the plane. If I want to look and feel *more intelligent,* I could bring my M.I.T. pen.

Advertisers have created specific strategies for imbuing specific traits for the brand they are selling into your brain as desirable. Victoria's Secret wasn't tested for sexy; it came up number one for glamorous. I suspect, but definitely don't know from personal experience, that wearing Victoria's Secret lingerie will make you feel more glamorous, feminine, and good-looking.

Victoria's Secret commercials and advertising often use powerful imagery of women walking the runway while wearing lingerie and angel wings. Everyone knows that there are lots of men and women watching those beautiful models walking the runway It would only make sense that a lot of women will either think consciously or nonconsciously something like, "I gotta get that."

Hypothetically, the brain sees the lingerie being worn by the Self and this probably causes that glamorous feeling to increase.

Is this only a signal to the Self?

Most people will not see the woman buying Victoria's Secret wearing the lingerie.

Most people will not be aware that she is wearing Victoria's Secret lingerie.

But somewhere in that brain is there a story line that has someone seeing her in the lingerie that night?

After all what is the alternative?

If she finds herself in the position of not having Victoria's Secret on and the moment happened to come along where she needed that glamour, femininity, and enhancement to her physical appearance, she'd certainly want to be ready. If she got to that moment and was caught wearing drab, boring Walmart underwear, what would that do to how she felt about herself, and what might not happen next?

I suspect that particular story line is running through the heads of many women who buy Victoria's Secret lingerie, and that is exactly what makes Victoria's Secret such a powerful brand.

The closer to naked you get, the more difficult it is to cloak reality.

Don't misunderstand. The story line is not necessarily a goal. It's some-thing that could transpire. The lingerie is simply being prepared for what *might* transpire.

Two dramatic Victoria's Secret commercials demonstrate the power of identification. Consider this most hypnotizing commercial. Five stunning models are walking down a hall. There is a row of plush chairs on either side of the hall, but no one is sitting in the chairs. Your brain will fill that in as you watch. The driving drumbeat captivates any attention not already gained. Then "5 Ways to be Incredible" flashes on the screen. (To watch this, go to YouTube and search for *Incredible by Victoria's Secret TV Commercial, Spring 2011 [Extended Cut].*)

I had to do further research, as the message to me was simply that there are five ways to be incredible and they are these girls. As a man I can do nothing but appreciate the close-up shots of the busts simply as a gift to me. There is no way I could see beyond that.

But to the woman watching the commercial, she sees what I don't notice or understand. There are five different kinds of bras here. One of them is called a "front close demi." Another is the "front close push-up."

These things I understand, but I have no identification with the need for the information.

And there is more that I don't see on the first take of the commercial.

What I do see is the models boldly, intensely walk forward. They own the room. They could have been shy, reserved, sweet, gentle. That's not these girls. They are intense. They would walk right over anyone standing in their way. They are wearing nothing but underwear and are in control of the room.

How would you feel and behave if you walked off an elevator wearing nothing but your underwear? Would you be in control of the room? Would you be the power broker?

That superhero strength from wearing the right lingerie is part of what the woman who wears VS gets from wearing VS. And they want their partner to know and sense that.

Most men or women walking off the elevator in their underwear would be having the nightmare of their life.

Can you imagine wearing something that would take your worst night-mare and turn it into your most desired dream?

Victoria's Secret boldly goes where no man has gone before. They recreate women in their own image, and it all works if you are wearing one of the 5 Ways to be Incredible.

VS offered another brilliant commercial that was just as hypnotic with a command: *"Give your angel a Christmas you'll never forget."* (You can watch this on YouTube by searching *Victoria's Secret Holiday 2010 TV Commercial [HD]*).

The woman watching the commercial knows she's your angel and now is certain that you (assuming you are her partner) consider her in the same way you considered the angels in the commercial.

These angels were given gifts by their guy (or gal).

VS is a master of not only brand identification but also permission.

As a man, in the presence of women, I need permission to stare, and I was just given that permission when I was ordered to buy what these angels are wearing and give it to my angel. How else would a dumb guy like me know what to buy my angel? If I don't watch, I'll never learn.

VS is telling the woman that you must let your guy observe this so he appreciates his woman . . . as his angel.

And who could argue?

But you work for the government, sell insurance, want to get the best deal in your next negotiation, and want to persuade the girl to go out with you.

What does VS have to do with any of these things?

It's a fair question after being spellbound by such a commercial. After all, to have the commercial running at the office could be considered harassment.

You have the same problems Victoria's Secret faces. Whether you are developing new products and services for people to use or you yourself are the product or the seller or marketer of the product, the problems are the same.

All we have discussed up to this point are the positive feelings and traits that can be experienced from an object. But understand that a positive object for one person could easily be a negative object for another person.

Also realize that the positive or negative impact an object has on a person is *different* for every person. Never assume that simply because you feel good about something that someone else will.

The person who was rejected by M.I.T. will hate you for placing an M.I.T. pen in their hand. The solution to this problem is to give people choices between objects you wish them to touch or use. Don't give them a pen to sign a document. Hold two pens in your hand and let them take the one they choose.

Your positive conversation about how you went to the university and graduated makes you feel good inside. It could turn the other person off because they had no money to go to school. Or perhaps they were abused at school. Never assume your specific experiences transfer. Your story of excitement can be someone else's hell.

A Strategy to Implement Invisible Influence

The lesson is that *you* bring attributes to the people who you interact with.

You transfer traits to people who decide to have a relationship of some kind with you.

You transfer traits to the girl you want to go out with you.

Do you have a plan as well constructed as the Victoria's Secret commercials?

The precise strategy VS uses is the strategy *you* must use as an individual, entrepreneur, salesperson, or marketer.

You are a brand. *People who know you have three words to describe you.* Perhaps they are feminine, glamorous, and good-looking. Perhaps they are smart, a leader, and elite. The descriptors aren't necessarily what you want them to be. At this moment those words are your brand image that you have developed for the past decade or two.

When you walk down the hallway with someone else, people who observe you walking with the guy or girl next to you take your brand image and transfer it to the innocent guy or girl and vice versa. That girl is signaling a message to everyone who can see her. That message is changed by walking next to you because she collects your traits, desirable or not.

The Identification Exercise

1. Write down 5 to 10 keywords or keyword phrases that other people would use to describe you, your looks, or your personality. If you are blisteringly hot in physical appearance, write that down. It is part of

your brand. It's what stands out to the world. If you are average in appearance, then it is not important. It's not part of your brand.

You might be branded by the world as being sweet, kind, loving, caring, hateful, evil, psychotic, hot, beautiful, a genius, sexy, good-looking, plain, boring, fat, gross, disgusting, unpleasant, rude, generous, empathetic, gentle, brash, or uncouth. Write the 5 to 10 words that you think people would use if they were going to rapidly describe you.

That is your current brand.

2. Next, write down the 5 to 10 words that you would strongly prefer people to use to describe you when they are talking about you.

Now what do you have to do to cause people to see you in the second image versus the first? If you can't change a word or phrase, erase it and add another phrase.

Think of it this way:

Why does someone want to come up to you and have a picture taken with you that they will then put up on their Facebook page?

The answer is the power of your current brand. If you have what they need, they'll do it.

3. If you do not have what they need, and they *do* have what you need, what are you going to do to acquire that?

Influence Factors Covered in This Chapter

Victoria's Secret models are *not* the brand in the first commercial. The brand is the lingerie and what the women are imbued with by the lingerie. Good-looking, feminine, glamorous.

1. VS models appear in control, bold, strong, wearing nothing but underwear. Through identification transference many women observing the commercial will want to feel that way as well.
2. The VS lingerie makes the model beautiful, not vice versa, is the message to the viewer. Wearing VS will make you good-looking, glamorous, feminine.

3. VS increases their market share by captivating the male viewer with the female viewer's permission. The message is "for your Angel at Christmas." Now the female viewer wants the male viewer to watch the commercial. And now the male viewer wants to sense and identify with the fact that lingerie makes the woman and not vice versa. The male now is more inclined to give his Angel VS. He does not know the branding of glamorous, good-looking, feminine. All he sees is what he can see. Beauty.

1 + 2 + 3 = you or your brand replace the lingerie. Your customer or the person you want to like you gains your brand traits by wearing or owning or using your product or services or being in a relationship with you. The product is a **signal** to *you* and to those your nonconscious brain wants to signal.

4. The mundane example of transferring brand character traits is the M.I.T. pen, which transfers feelings of intelligence, leadership to those who believe they cannot change who they are as people. Your mundane product can be branded similarly. So can you.
5. People are influenced by objects. Place a bag, a pen, a VS bag in someone's hands, and their feelings and emotions change. Be *very* careful and intentional about what you place in someone's hands. Remember, *everything* influences. The M.I.T. pen changed people's feelings of intelligence and sense of leadership ability.
6. No words are required to cause influence and change. An object can be far more powerful than any word ever could be.
7. Become aware of objects on your desk, your coffee table, your wall, your refrigerator, and ponder how they might influence others both positively and negatively. Objects include books and magazines. Because books and magazines have both imagery and text on the covers, it's very possible that these may be objects that carry a lot of magic. You should always be pondering what feelings might be triggered in others by the objects in your midst.

Remember, every branding process works similarly to every other branding process. This is true whether you are thinking of your mom as a brand, or your daughter as a brand, or your friend, or your neighbor. There are a few words and characteristics that you have on your tongue tip that immediately describe this person. The same is true about the car you drive, the ketchup you use, the soda you drink, the wine you pour.

Brands are about imbuing you (or someone or something) with traits you or they desire to be seen as possessing and then making them unmistakably transferable to the individual using your product, service, or associating with you.

Think about what *you* bring to the people who hang out with you.

What do you bring and spread to the people who stand by you, walk with you, or have lunch with you?

The Initial Identification Exercise

Now, imagine you are walking down the hallway in a location where no one knows you. No one has seen you before.

What words do people use to describe you?

That's your first impression.

That impression often becomes your brand.

So you might want to buy Lucky jeans.

The key point here goes far beyond making a good first impression. You want to have a look, an image, a reputation, a brand for your Self of your choosing. Don't leave these life-changing variables to fate.

Brand you, your product, your service with great intention and purpose. Make it so people identify you in a specific way when communicating about you with others.

Always keep in mind precisely what it will mean to someone who is using your pen or your product or walking down the hall with you—and what it will mean to those who are watching the other person.

Are observers thinking, "Why would she walk with that idiot?" or, "Ah, she's lucky, she's walking with him."

Do their nonconscious evaluations say, "She must be smarter than I thought if she's with him."

And if you are doing any kind of intentional influencing, make sure that the things you touch, the things you choose to have other people look at are all prepared with great preparation. Do you want to have the person sign with the M.I.T. pen or the ballpoint pen? This will change with each context of course. An M.I.T. pen in some parts of town will carry the opposite effect as it did in the study. It will be like poison in many contexts.

*So think carefully what **your** customer, client, friend, or potential date are going to get from everything they touch that you touched.*

3

Kim Kardashian's Connectors

Surprise? You have them all.

You know Kim. She's the girl who married the tall guy and then two months later they went their separate ways, with the divorce proceedings lasting longer than the engagement and marriage combined. Her mother is one of the truly brilliant contemporary marketers, and Kim has learned well from her mother.

Some of what Kim does is not replicable. She's good-looking and has a body that doesn't stop.

Some of what she does is replicable. She works incredibly hard. She tolerates public pressure in a way that makes politicians envious. She gets marketing and in particular branding.

She's 30 and has 16,000,000 Twitter followers. That places her tenth on the planet.

Some of what the Kardashians do as a family is nothing short of brilliant.

You don't need to watch their popular television shows to learn this.

So what are they doing right that you are probably doing wrong? You're probably trying to use an "off-the-shelf solution" for a start.

"Kevin, I have a question. I need to persuade buyers. Will it work, if I say . . . .'"

Or "My company currently does X and Y, and it's not working. I'm thinking of making a change, inducing reciprocity, training my sales staff on expectancy, and using social proof as the final nail."

30

In Direct Marketing you can attempt to influence with a script. That could be online or using long-form copy sent by mail. In either of these scenarios you *can* create an optimal presentation with specific factors of influence.

In every other scenario, every single presentation or communication you enter into must absolutely utilize different factors of influence, particularly Invisible Influence. The Kim Kardashian Connectors can be applied in every persuasive communication you have with another person.

Some will be completely new to you. Some defy intuition. Some are just like you thought they would be, had you thought of them. There are many factors of influence that determine whether someone will say yes or no. The most excellent thing about the factors of influence is that there are many, many of them.

That means there is a great deal to learn.

And it means that as you learn each new factor you become more influential, more persuasive. It's like walking into your home and flipping on one light switch at a time. Most people just flip on one or two light switches and thus have very little light. They have very little success at captivating, mastering connection, persuading one, or influencing thousands.

In this chapter you will learn **unique** triggers.

Unique triggers are **specific** to the individual you are attempting to influence. In each case the triggers engender identification.

The specific triggers I'm introducing here are clustered under the name, *The Kim Kardashian Connectors.*

Triggers can include words and phrases, sentences and chapters, like primes, models, gestures, movement, color, drives, contexts, stimulus-response buttons, and on and on.

A factor of influence that could enhance the result of an interaction to the tune of 1 to 10 percent can be dramatic. The scientist, the salesperson, or marketer reads these numbers as "statistically significant" or meaning "substantially greater profits."

Even a 1 to 2 percent weight in your favor can tip the balance to a yes instead of a no.

Your Average Joe wants one thing that will cause the gal to say yes. And that's why he is average. He obviously doesn't want to work too hard.

The girl doesn't like lazy. Prestige comes with status.

Status comes from mastery and recognition from others.

You don't get those by being lazy.

Never be average or worse. It's as simple as that.

The sharp individual wants to master as many factors as they can collect so that it's highly unlikely they'll hear "no."

The actions of persuasion rarely include a generic sentence one can parrot that is then useful to all people everywhere. A few notable exceptions might be:

"I was wrong."

"I'm sorry."

"You are the best."

There aren't many others. If there were strings of sentences and scripts you could mouth that had worked in the past, you'd eventually see them in all advertising and their effect would in time be diluted to the point they had no effect.

Imagine that every website online used a *BUY NOW!* button that looked the same as every other one and that every single button was red and had 16-point font letters and . . . you get the idea. What would happen? Would that cause everyone's sales to increase? You know that's not possible, so what must occur?

Think about it.

If every single human on earth were selling Product X using Sales Letter Y because they had been proven the best, what would happen?

It would cause sales to evaporate. *Everyone would go broke.* The perfect proven combination now fails every time.

This is why the more people who use System Q or Sales Letter Y or Approach X, the more that system will fail.

Once the girl has heard the same exact words from 10 consecutive guys, she'll realize that something is wrong. She is hanging around average and that's less than boring.

Exact words will ultimately fail.

If people don't consider something they identify with as unique and exclusive to some "in" group, it will fail.

People are identity driven and stimulated or triggered by what resonates with them with what says, "That's me."

Back to Kim Kardashian and her family brand and what influences her, her family, and her fans.

Kris Humphries (basketball player) in one way was a predictable choice for Kim Kardashian to marry, at a subconscious level.

"K" works in the Kardashian family.

To a lesser extent "H" works there as well.

Here's what I mean . . . and how you can utilize a powerful and little known factor of persuasion.

Names and letters are powerful focal points of identification, and Kim Kardashian is a powerful girl in a brand-name family.

Kim's name, *Kim Kardashian,* is not only her personal identity; it is a brand name for products and business. The logo of all things *Kim Kardashian* is the reverse K and forward K. It's familiar and recognizable to most women under 35 years old.

Let's look at influence triggers in perhaps the most important decision you'll make: naming your children.

In the 1970s, Robert Kardashian, famed for being one of O.J. Simpson's trial attorneys, married an attractive gal named Kris.

No surprise there.

K's (Kardashian in this case) marry other K's (Kris) with a greater frequency than they statistically would be expected to. After Kris, Kim's even moved on with Kanye West, but I can't tell you if K.W. will work out any better than K.H.

J's, L's, and M's marry K's with greater frequency as well. That doesn't seem intuitive, but in real life, your locker, for example, is next to other people with letters close to yours in your last name. So I ended up hanging out with Higginbothom, Hofftiezer, Jacobsen, Linde, and Lundgren a great deal. You did the same thing.

When you registered for classes at the university you went to the H–L line (or whatever the first initial of your last name is).

We are divided by names and letters in more situations than you can instantly guess.

Robert and Kris had three children, and they were all named with a "K" family identity: Kim, Kourtney, Khloe.

Robert and Kris had a son and named him . . . Robert. People love to give their name to their children.

I married a girl with the initials K.K.

Her middle name?

The same as my mother's first name.

Ironic or the way life often plays out? I remember that striking a chord when I learned that piece of information. A most attractive girl and then some.

Meanwhile Robert Kardashian passes away, leaving his family in a most interesting and unusual way to Bruce Jenner, one of the greatest athletes in history. (J is right next to K in the alphabet, of course.)

Kris and Bruce then went on to have Kendall and Kylie.

Today several television shows revolve around the daily happenings of this family, the highest rated being *Keeping Up with the Kardashians.*

Letters become representations of ourselves. Or more precisely, our *Selves.* That K is powerful in ways you might have only imagined prior to today. And it goes further!

The sound of the "kuh" or the visual K is all it takes to trigger the feeling "just like me."

If your name begins with either the initial K or the sound, "kuh" then something positive is going to happen when you see or hear that letter K or sound "kuh." This is true for any letter of the alphabet or any sound.

People choose to marry others with similar sounding first or last names:

Eric marries Erica.
Charles marries Charlotte.

Marriage, a decision and choice you would think would be thoroughly considered, is quite often the result of an impulse trigger.

Most people attempt to build rapport in very simplistic terms. I've written extensively in other books on this important topic and won't elaborate here.

People can synchronize body postures, body language, and vocal qualities to generate that "sorta like me" feeling.

But "K" is not "sorta"; "K" *is me* . . . if your name is Kim or Kevin.

You respond very favorably to most things that remind you of you.

How so?

Here are a couple of examples of the power of these unseen factors on where people choose to live:

Louisiana has more than its statistical share of Louises than it should.
Florence has more than its statistical share of Florences than it should.

People choose to live on streets whose name matches their own.

Mr. Washington moves to Washington Street more often than Jefferson Street.

People often move to cities with numbers in the city name that match their birth date numbers, like Two Harbors, Minnesota or Three Forks, Montana, for example.

People with the name Georgia do indeed move to Georgia more than they statistically should.[1]

But the influence of names and letters goes beyond just your name.

I was looking at luxury homes all over the Midwest. One home was on a street named Coffee. It didn't even dawn on me until I was going to place an offer. Down to four homes, and one was on a street with the word that is often associated with my name by people all over the world: every Monday I release an e-zine called *Coffee with Kevin Hogan*.

Ultimately what did I do?

Again, unaware until long after the fact, I bought a home in a location that began with one of the initials in my name.

Coincidence? Perhaps.

About 10 years ago I was looking for a home and found the right one. Then I didn't buy it. It was on McCool Avenue. I kid you not. It was the right home, for sure. But on McCool? For some reason I started to find things wrong with the house and location after I had already decided to buy it. "McCool" just wasn't cool.

Have you ever bought something or ceased from buying something because of its name?

Do you have an Apple iPhone or an iPad?

Would you have bought it if it was called a Radish iPhone or a Celery iPad?

Imagine someone who buys a Maserati. That is one cool car.

What if it was named Broccoli or Asparagus?

People, when asked to trust their feelings, preferred products whose first letters matched first letters of their names. For example:

Allan likes Almond Joy.

Nick likes Nutrageous.

---

[1] B.W. Pelham, M.C. Mirenberg, and J.T. Jones, "Why Susie sells seashells by the Seashore: Implicit Egotism and Major Life Decisions," *Journal of Personality and Social Psychology* 82, no. 4 (2002): 469–487.

What's in Your Cupboard?

Having various pet names for products or services could pay off handsomely.

Do this now.

Write down the initials of your name. (Print, not manuscript.)

Now look around you. Where else do you see those initials?

How do you feel about each of those things in comparison with other things nearby?

Most people never have consciously considered this so you can test this with any group of people you come into contact with.

I want you to begin developing that creative self within you so that you can think of dozens of applications for every factor of influence you find here.

The factors of influence accumulate and continue to be effective because almost no one uses them. Almost no one is conscious of them as being influential. And that very fact keeps them consistently valuable to you.

For example: If I still gave out business cards, I'd have 26 cards prepared for the 26 letters.

"But how can I change my name, my company name, or the names of my products and books?"

Obviously that's not practical, most of the time.

Here is how I would utilize one of the Kim Kardashian Connectors with something as simple as business cards.

I'd begin by having a short message on my card that utilizes initials to match your customer's. I would have my URL and nothing else.

Please note: I'm making these little messages up on the fly. You'll take time and do it with more precision and flare.

Card One you will give to the individual with first or last name beginning with "A":

An Amazing Adventure Awaits You!
www.kevinhogan.com

That card would be given to Allen, Art, and other people whose names begin with "A." And if you don't have "A" as an initial, you might think, "Well that seems ridiculous." And you'd be required to reevaluate that opinion *once you feel how strong the bond is between your initials and you.*

Card Two for the individual with first or last name beginning with "B":

Brilliant Experiences Begin Here!
www.kevinhogan.com

That card would go to Bob, Barry, Bill, and other people whose names began with the letter "B."

Delivering Both Daring and Dignified Designs
www.kevinhogan.com

And so on.

In about one hour you will go through the alphabet and come up with 26 cards. And what about those Q, X, Y, Z names?

The "Letter/Initial Effect" is even more profound with people who have less frequently observed letters in their name.

What are other simple ways you can take advantage of the Letter/Initial Effect?

Whether it's on invoices, envelopes, or Christmas cards, artfully and elegantly placed "letter personalization" will be experienced as a trigger that strikes a very, very strong and positive chord in the other person's mind.

The identity connection of initials, letters, and sounds is so powerful it influences your future career and where you will live.

I'm curious, when you look at it, do you find you or your spouse's initial(s) on the street sign your residence is on? What about the city? State?

Have you ever considered how you want to protect the child who shares your name when the mother is yelling at that child in the store?

Frankly, it doesn't matter as much (to me) when I'm out at the store if a mom over there is yelling at Quincy. But please do *not* yell at Kevin: he's a good kid.

Does it bug you just a bit when someone with your name commits a crime and the name is in big letters in the newspaper?

And while we are deliberating on initials and names, it should become obvious that what you name your child will influence their future in a dramatic fashion.

To be blunt, the name you give your child will be a lifelong experience for that child, so don't blow it.

There are two ways this plays out.

The first is the name itself.

Now here is how powerful identity can be.

If you named your child Michael, you picked the single most popular name you could have chosen. Good job. You can't go wrong there.

Half as many people have the name David. That's still absolutely fine. Good choice.

But what if you decided to be creative and give your child a name like Kareem, Alec, Malcolm, Ernest?

Not so good.

In fact, you have a lot of making up to do because those names are the least popular of all names.

"Ah, but that's what makes him special, Kevin. I didn't want him to be like everyone else!"

And he won't be.

He's much more likely to end up in prison. The research showing the connection between juvenile delinquency, criminal activity, and PNI (Popularity of Name Index) developed by David E. Kalist and Daniel Y. Lee at Shippenburg University is clear-cut on that.[2]

(And do not notice that David and Daniel did the research. Certainly a coincidence.)

And you must be thinking, "but Kareem Abdul Jabbar, Alec Guiness, Alec Baldwin, Ernest Hemingway, Malcolm X. That's some pretty good company."

Not in the twenty-first century.

It *was* pretty good company. Adolph worked pretty well in most countries until about 1935ish.

Do you have friends and relatives who you care about?

Don't let them make a disastrous mistake. I've stuck my nose into people's business on this subject many times over the years. Even if they resent you, you probably saved their kid and a lot of phone calls to you for support 16 years later!

Although the first initials (K.H. for me, what are yours?) are the most important to a person, K.L.H. is absolutely identifiable as "me," and I, like you, have a preference for *all* of the letters in all three of my names. K-E-V-I-N. You also have a preference for people who have those letters in their name (first and last).

---

[2] D.E. Kalist, and D.Y. Lee, "First Names and Crime: Does Unpopularity Spell Trouble?" *Social Science Quarterly* 90 (January 2009): 39–49.

You particularly notice less common letters like "V" and "K" when you unconsciously compare your name to another's.

Does this mean that your best friend won't have a name that's completely different than yours?

Of course not, but it means it is *less likely* that they will.

Have you ever thought, "She spells her name wrong," or "It's weak."

Her name is Chloe. Yours is Khloe.

Her name is Lori. Yours is Laurie.

Her name is Kayla. It's Cayla.

And so on.

When you have the spelling one way and theirs is another, they are now inferior to you in this respect.

You're Bob, he's Robert?

"Pretentious."

You're Phil, he's Philip?

"He's probably a Brit."

You're Alex and she's Alexandra?

"Get over yourself."

You're Katherine and she's Kathy?

"Girl has no class."

Fleeting thoughts that you now recognize you've had hundreds of times in your life.

The influence of names and letters goes even further.

People with the name Dennis are more likely to be dentists when compared to the rest of the population.

Raymond is more likely to be a radiologist when compared with the rest of the population.

And we know that people with the same last name as a profession or trade generally are more likely to do business in that trade than the general population as a whole.

So a man with the last name Carpenter is more likely than you would statistically anticipate to be a carpenter.

You'd probably be right if you thought Mr. Mason was more likely to be in masonry.

Hardware store owners? Their names that start with "H" were 80 percent greater than those that started with "R."

Roofers? Those with names beginning with "R" were 70 percent more often found than those with names beginning with "H."

The KK Factors are some of the most reliable triggers in influence.

Triggers that relate to the identity of an individual are all but certain to have a positive influence on the outcome of an event or transaction.

It might be **the difference** between yes and no, and of course it might not be as well. But it will be a significant factor.

Now let me ask you a question: Do you like your name and initials?

Most people do. But not those given names that suck.

And, as the research has shown, sometimes you like the initials enough to influence other important behaviors. For example, Jack is more likely to move to Jacksonville and marry Jackie than is Philip, who is more likely to move to Philadelphia and marry Phyllis.

Scientists call this phenomenon the "name-letter effect" and say that it is influential enough to encourage the pursuit of name-resembling life outcomes and partners.

However, if you like your name too much, you might be in trouble.

Leif Nelson at the University of California, San Diego, and Joseph Simmons from Yale University found that *liking your own name sabotages success for people whose initials match negative performance labels.*[3]

In their first study, Nelson and Simmons investigated the effect of name resemblance on batters' strikeouts. In baseball, strikeouts are recorded using the letter "K."

After analyzing major league baseball players' performance spanning 93 years, the researchers found that batters whose names began with K struck out at a higher rate than the remaining batters.

In a second study, Nelson and Simmons investigated the phenomenon in school:

> *Students whose names began with C or D earned lower GPAs than students whose names began with A or B.*

How else do names influence behavior?

The first letter of your childhood surname determines much about your consumer behavior as an adult.

Why are some people more likely than others to wait in line overnight to buy a just-released book or to queue up for the new iPad?

---

[3] L. Nelson and J. Simmons, "Moniker Maladies: When Names Sabotage Success," *Psychological Science* 14 (November 2007): 106–110.

"The tendency to act quickly to acquire items such as those mentioned is related to the first letter of one's childhood surname," write Kurt A. Carlson (Georgetown University) and Jacqueline M. Conard (Belmont University).[4]

These authors examined how quickly adults responded to opportunities to acquire items of value to them. ***They found that the later in the alphabet people's childhood surnames were, the faster those consumers responded to purchase opportunities.***

The "last-name effect" occurred when the items were real (basketball tickets, cash, and wine) or hypothetical (sale on a backpack).

The effect occurred only with childhood surnames, not names that had changed due to marriage. Children with last names that fall late in the alphabet are often at the end of lines or at the back of the class.

"The idea holds that children develop time-dependent responses based on the treatment they receive," Carlson and Conrad explained. (Notice Carlson and Conrad . . . another coincidence, I'm certain.)

"In an effort to account for these inequities, children late in the alphabet will move quickly when last name isn't a factor; they will 'buy early.' Likewise, those with last names early in the alphabet will be so accustomed to being first that individual opportunities to make a purchase won't matter very much; they will 'buy late.'

"The last-name effect is especially important to retailers and salespeople because customer names are easy for marketers to obtain and because there are many decisions in which the decision is not whether to buy, but when to buy," C and C wrote in 2011.

Whether it's shopping at a clearance sale, choosing a seat to hear live music, or shopping for produce at a farmers' market, late alphabet consumers want to make sure they're the first in line.

As much as your name and your initials are part of your identity, ***your signature is significantly more important.***

In fact, your signature *means* a great deal because you are warranting something almost every single time you sign your name.

What Does Signing Your Name Mean in the Selling Process?

For years salespeople have tried to get a customer to sign a document, any document, to unconsciously sway the person to purchase whatever they are selling.

---

[4] K. A. Carlson and J. M. Conard, "The Last Name Effect: How Last Name Influences Acquisition Timing," *Journal of Consumer Research* 38, no. 2 (January 2011).

Does this work? Does the customer's identity really get wrapped up in the signature?

How could that be?

The research has been done.

Here is the answer.

Signing your name on the dotted line heightens your sense of self and leads to purchase behavior that affirms your self-identity, according to a new study in the *Journal of Consumer Research*. But signing can reduce engagement in consumers who don't identify strongly with a product or category.

"Although there are numerous ways in which people may present their identity to others, signing one's name has distinct legal, social, and economic implications," say the researchers, Keri L. Kettle and Gerald Häubl (University of Alberta). The act of signing also has implications in the marketplace.[5]

In one experiment, consumers were asked to either sign or print their name (in an ostensibly unrelated task) before visiting a sporting goods store to purchase a pair of running shoes. "For consumers who closely associate their identity with running, compared to printing their name, providing their signature before entering the store caused an increase in the number of running shoes they tried on and in the amount of time they spent in the store," K and H write.

Signing their name had the opposite effect on people who did not associate their identity with running; they spent less time in the store and tried on fewer shoes.

In another study, consumers were asked to make a series of product choices after either **signing or printing** their names. *Consumers who signed were more likely to choose an option that was popular with a social group they belong to. The tendency was stronger when consumers chose in a product category that signaled their identity to others (a jacket) than when they selected in a category that does not signal their identity (toothpaste).*

The study has implications for retailers and consumers, the authors explain. For instance, a retailer might ask shoppers to sign their names after completing a survey, to enter a prize drawing, or enroll in a loyalty program, since it is likely to lead consumers who identify closely with the store's products to become more engaged.

However, such signature interventions should be used cautiously, as signing tends to reduce engagement in consumers who lack such identification.

---

[5] K. L. Kettle and G. Häubl, "The Signature Effect: Signing Influence Consumption-Related Behavior by Priming Self-Identity," *Journal of Consumer Research* 38 (October 2011): 474–489.

"Although a signature does not necessarily imply commitment, it does always represent one's identity. Because consumers sign (or can be asked to do so) in many consumption contexts, it is important to develop a deeper understanding of how producing one's signature influences behavior," K and H conclude.

Identity

The Kardashian Identity is not much different than my identity or yours. Understanding the power of your customers' and clients' identities now causes you to intentionally take that identity into consideration.

To do otherwise would make no sense.

4 | Your Self and Others

Ever see someone . . . well . . . you know . . . pinch her butt?

Right now you're probably laughing, smiling, cringing, or remembering when you pinched her butt.

I remember when I've had my butt pinched, and I can tell you that every time I was thrilled someone found me pinchable.

Now, let's take a look inside the brain because a great deal has just transpired in the last three lines of text.

Your brain almost certainly saw him pinch her butt. That is the stereotypical or "most likely" picture stored in your brain. It's more than a prediction; it's an "instant dub in" to an ambiguous picture. But alas, you are mistaken. The culprit wasn't a he. It was actually a "she."

Someone pinched her butt.

Wow.

The brain engages in all kinds of cool processes to actually give you a movie or picture of something that you think you just saw. But this was more than a simple case of mistaken identity. Your brain created a man out of thin air and placed his two fingers at her butt then constructed the man to go with the fingers, after which a judgment was placed upon said man.

Yet there was no man to judge.

The brain performs all of this in a fraction of a second. It fills in all the gaps out there in life with whatever it selects out of the brain's clip art file.

That's the world you and I walk around in every single day. Reality plus clip art filler. And everyone has a different clip art file that matches his or her prior experiences.

When you saw "someone" pinch the girl's butt, you saw a man.

Before going on, do understand that you now have a vivid example of how people can be made to believe something that is not true. You can easily cause a person to believe something that is not real.

Here's what is even more remarkable.

The image or movie you saw in your mind caused you to have a feeling and a reaction.

You laughed.

You smiled.

You were disgusted.

You were irritated.

Perhaps you were even outraged that I would be smiling that the man (who doesn't exist) pinched the girl's butt. Your brain instantly developed both a feeling and a reaction about the image, plus a judgment about Kevin because he smiled that the girl's butt was pinched by that guy.

Except that it wasn't a guy.

But let's say that it was. Let's just say for the sake of discussion that the person you saw pinch the girl's butt was indeed male. You still had a reaction to the scene and then a stronger reaction to my reported reaction.

Now, let's suppose the man is her husband and that the girl and guy engage in mutual butt pinches with some regularity. Now your judgment would be very different.

Remember that every time you see, hear, or read something.

You have a grossly incomplete picture.

Your brain fills in every missing or ambiguous image that is not painted for you. Then it fills in emotions, judgments, beliefs.

Then the brain's wiring fires off past reactions to similar experiences.

Then you see my reaction, which was probably different than what I reported it to be.

Then I tell you what you saw wasn't what you read.

And *that* fact creates another set of feelings and emotions.

Perhaps you felt sheepish.

Maybe you grinned and thought, "Aw that Kevin! He got me on that one."

Perhaps you thought something unkind about me. Don't worry, I don't take it personally because *you* didn't actually *think anything*.

Let me explain the science behind that statement.

Who Are You?

Inside your brain there are dozens of processing algorithms, dozens of "employees of you," which take care of thousands of tasks.

You project several different selves "in the brain" that are activated in different situations and environments.

The day you were born you began absorbing all kinds of new information into your brain.

Your brain and body had spent perhaps nine months tucked safely away in your mom's uterus. You collected information in there, but the new world, the world where there is sunlight and crisp sounds and sensations, brought a new meaning to the word *stimulus*.

It didn't take too many days before you were able to distinguish faces you liked from faces you didn't like. You were able to know a smile from a frown. You were able to track people moving around.

For a little while your neural net would expand. Your potential for learning and soaking in new info got bigger. But then the whole thing got unwieldy and the number of connections in your brain actually started to reduce by quite a lot.

Early in life children aren't completely familiar with the notion that they are a separate object in the environment. They feel very connected to everything around them.

In those early years there are repeating experiences that create expectations of the experiences. These repeating experiences revolve around people, places, things, and feelings. Sometimes these people, places, things, and feelings become part of their inner world. They become part of the person other people see as "you."

Your life experience around your mother was likely very different than it was with your father. If both parents were in the home, you responded differently to each parent. Each parent fulfilled different needs and wants. Each communicated in different tones and facial expressions. Each parent generated different feelings within you. Your parents, or the adults and children you grew up with, became parts of you.

Clearly your behavior was different around your father than your mother. It was different around your mother than it was your babysitter. It was different around the babysitter than it was the cat. Your behavior was different around the cat than it was your sister. You behaved differently in the kitchen than in your bedroom. Behavioral patterns and your internal feelings created many unique experiential patterns that would generally last a lifetime.

These behavioral patterns included the ability to predict what other people, animals, or things would do in certain places because those things had happened so many times. Your brain carried around your mom, dad, brother, cat, the kitchen, and all these other things. You had unique relationships with all of them. Different feelings engendered different behaviors, and different behaviors engendered different feelings.

When your mom came home after being away, you either ran up to her or didn't care that much that she had returned. When you saw your cat, you either ran to the cat or didn't care that much.

All of these people, places, and things literally became a part of you.

Quite often in your early life you'd experience fear or pain. You developed consistent reactions and responses to pains and fears. There were places you learned to hate and places you learned to love. Coping with those places and people created lifelong patterns that generalized to similar situations as you got older.

These patterns eventually firmed up and became predictable and distinguishable from other patterns that were triggered in other settings, contexts, and with other people.

You can recognize these patterns, for example, when you return home at Christmas and you see that all of the 40-year-old "kids" still behave the same around the 65-year-old mom and dad. The "kids" regress to their preteen years in their behavior with each other in predictable fashion. Their language use changes, as does their speaking volume, their bossiness or submissiveness, and so on. The family easily fits into their old roles in an almost instant fashion. Spouses and friends find this strange because they see you behave completely differently (in most cases) from your day-to-day life as an adult in your own home.

The patterns are generated by vast clusters of neurons that interact with each other and the environment. Hypnotherapists refer to these as *parts* of someone. Psychoanalysts refer to them as *ego states*. Scientists refer to them as *subroutines* or *selves*.

Most people are surprised to find out just how many subroutines, just how many employees are working for you on any given day.

In some cases I like to refer to them as "employees of The Self" because they take care of business while you mentally check out.

Regardless of the label, it describes roughly the same thing. There is a part of the person that is clearly evident for all to see that is much less frequently seen in other circumstances. Some scientists believe that many of these selves have personalities or personality traits. Others don't. One thing is certain: they all direct different kinds of behavior when they are at the forefront of the personality.

Attempting to influence someone without knowing which self is in charge is more complex than influencing someone when you know what role the person is in.

When people later say, "I changed my mind," they have no idea how literally true that is. You should always anticipate people changing their minds along the way. This is why oscillation between yes and no occurs. One part or more is in favor of a proposal and another is not.

Most behavior from these subpersonalities is generally seen to be protecting some interest of the individual. Parts of the human mind are often in conflict, and these conflicts can make coming to a decision very difficult in many situations.

Think of those subpersonalities or subroutines as employees in a grocery store. The processes are partial representations of the store management or the store ambience, but the employee is by no means the company.

But these employees weren't hired. They were *born* in the brain. You didn't create the jobs. The employees found the work and took specific jobs as life situations were experienced.

The employees include Mom, Dad, Uncle Joe, your babysitter, your first-grade teacher, the minister, and maybe even your cat.

At any given time there are subroutine processes going on in your brain over which you have (almost) no control. Pictures, movies, sounds, and feelings are pushed into consciousness by these processes.

Your process is not you. I don't hold you at fault for the parts of your brain that instantly fill in ambiguous images and paint a picture that probably makes good sense to you, but bears no resemblance to reality.

You have nothing to apologize for.

They Don't Know What They're Thinking About

The vast majority of the time you aren't thinking anything. You simply have images, pictures, sounds, feelings all squirted up into your thinking brain from below by your employees. It's just like they were squeezing ketchup and mustard containers.

Most people rarely think or analyze any of the stuff that comes into the brain from below. It's just there.

It doesn't mean anything, beyond what one of the "employees of you" has squished into your mind.

The vast majority of these images, feelings, and experiences are never considered by the conscious mind in any way.

But . . .

The processes that slide these vivid images, or movies, into your brain typically don't simply remove them rapidly. Like most employees, they tend to be only average at their job. They leave stuff lying around and may not pull the movie until you've actually watched it, unconsciously acted upon it, or talked about it. In fact sometimes they replay the same soundtracks over and over.

The Nonstop Soundtrack in Your Head

Remember having a song stuck in your head that you have a hard time getting rid of? Write down why you think you might not have control of that song. How is it turned on when none of the others are on? Why is it you don't hear two songs at the same time? Why can't you shut it off? Why can't you change the song even when you start singing a different song to drive that song out of your mind?

This happened yesterday with me.

My brain was playing "Paradise by the Dashboard Light" by Meat Loaf for around two hours. I was working on writing my latest issue of *Coffee with Kevin Hogan* and was really tired of thinking about being barely 17 and barely dressed . . . or maybe I wasn't tired of it, but I was ready for turning 18 and playing some guitar or something different.

I love Meat Loaf, but I decided to take control of my own brain and I went upstairs and popped in an Elvis concert DVD. Meat Loaf instantly yielded to Elvis and my brain was fully engaged into "Just Pretend," "I Just Can't Help Believing," and "Something."

Relieved, I returned to my couch and coffee table, lay down, got ready to work on *Coffee with Kevin Hogan* . . . And then the brain kicked into the baseball radio broadcast in "Paradise by the Dashboard Light." "Stop right there! Before we . . . " I gave in. My brain *really* wanted to be 17, so let it be 17 and it played on for the rest of the day. There are worse ages to be. It could have gotten stuck at 12 . . . *that* was a very bad year.

Judging Squirts and Splashes

You don't simply dub in the movie and see the images that are squirted into your brain; you form judgments about those movies.

In other words, you might have seen some guy pinch her butt. As we've discussed, that never happened, but you still have an emotional feeling about it.

Right?

No.

You have no feeling about it at all.

A process in your brain squirted in all the dub and then *another process* came into judgment on the new movie that you actually saw.

Let's say someone was appalled that "he" pinched her butt.

Aside from the fact that he was quite innocent because he was a she, a judgment was laid out.

"That's cute."

"That's terrible."

"That's chauvinistic."

"That's wrong."

"That's funny."

"I wish I could do that."

"She does have a nice butt."

You didn't actually think of your response. An employee pushed it into your brain as well.

And it caused you to feel whatever reaction you had. And in general because of other processes of the brain, you don't question your feelings. You trust them. You never stand back and realize that the feelings were simply given to you by an employee of you. You simply *felt*.

You felt it so you must be right.

And then your conscious mind needs to justify being right.

Going forward from today, you'll find yourself acting on these feelings with disquieting regularity.

When people say, "Trust your feelings," to both of you it sounds exactly like, "You are competent," but what you are being prompted to go with is the first impulse created by the most activated employee, the one who managed to squirt his ketchup into your brain first. Knowing that, you now understand your impulses are no more than whims.

And that is how most people decide yes or no, or a or b.

When influencing others, you ideally have the right "part" or "subroutine" available. You can then communicate with the person knowing that the available subroutine, or part of the person, is prepared to react to you.

A parental part is very different than that of a lover.

The lover will take great risks to achieve what his or her love desires. The parental part will take no such risks and will do everything it can to keep the self and others secure.

As you can see parts or "employees" are going to come into conflict. The same is true on your computer. There are programs that you can't run at the same time. You can't run *Camtasia* with certain other programs on your computer. Many programs interfere with others. The same is true for the "employees of you."

Although they all tend to do a pretty good job, they all have strengths and weaknesses. They've had no training except personal experience.

Let's imagine an individual had a parent die when he was a teenager or younger. A subroutine develops to protect the self from harm, including the emotional harm of other people dying in the future. This can cause what other people consider strange behavior.

A friend of mine called the other day. "Kevin, am I freaking my son out by talking about what happens if I die?"

Her mom had died of a vicious case of cancer at age 12. As you would expect, a subroutine had developed around this fact. It always does. Always. Depending on how the person survived the initial experience, the person will anticipate people responding in a similar way when other people leave or die in her life.

And the person will also tend to replicate experiences in the future.

For example, if Mom died of cancer at age 12, then the person will perform specific behaviors to try and stop other people from leaving or dying. They might obsess about health or practical issues that in other families were never considered.

This person might buy life insurance at age 30 (as I did) when the probability of death is perhaps less than 1 in 5,000. But because the experience has happened to them, they will be much more careful and plan around likely or unlikely events with much more fervor.

To exploit a life experience like this is something that would disturb me greatly. However, to cause someone to perform useful behaviors by spinning the person to this specific subroutine could be of inestimable value.

You've probably said, "I haven't made up my mind," or "I can't make up my mind," or "My mind isn't made up yet," or "I'll make up my mind tomorrow."

Wanna bet?

These feelings and notions are common for you and me, along with everyone else in the world, because parts are often in great conflict over what and how much they should be squirting into the person's brain.

People feel overwhelmed specifically because of these conflicts. Many parts are pushing a great deal of information to the surface of consciousness, causing literally too many feelings and too much information for you (or anyone else) to adequately process.

Because parts or subroutines are notoriously stubborn when it comes to their jobs, they tend to keep pushing intentions into the brain until a decision is made or, more often than not, not made.

Unfortunately decisions are slow to come because of such great conflicting imagery!

So the protective part tells the person to avoid the potential new lover for fear of an insecure family situation. Meanwhile the part that is concerned with acquiring new or fresh love is sending up images of good times, excitement, and romance. These two parts alone can go into conflict for days, weeks, months, and even years.

The easiest way to move a person from no to maybe is activating the right part to generate a negotiation with the part that is saying, no.

Ultimately it's generally important to convince the dissenting subroutine that a yes decision will actually bring great benefit to the self.

Here's an example:

The girl wants to go out with the guy, but she also has this feeling of intimidation or fear. The astute guy senses this and says something like, "Hey, why don't you invite Sarah to come along with us tonight. I'll take you both out to eat. And if Sarah wants to bring somebody, she can, too."

This accomplishes quelling the anxiety for the vigilant part, as well as allowing the party animal out to play.

If the subroutine is shown to have been correct and it allowed a yes decision when it should have kept squirting images for no, then of course you can assume the future will cause even greater conflict.

The activity below the surface of consciousness is typically quite high. Thousands or millions of switches can be flipped up or down in a second, and images are created at high speeds that aren't controllable by the conscious mind.

If you remember that you are dealing with a multitude of possible decision makers within an individual, you have a great advantage.

Is this advantage *over* the other person?

Of course it is, if you choose that route.

But your advantage could be in helping that person. People who understand the underground of the brain will be most valuable in influencing others.

5 | Your Trusted Self

Over the course of your life, you've developed many distinct "parts" or "employees," right? Pick your favorite descriptor. They are used interchangeably.

The "you" of you is the CEO of the company. You are influenced by the employees. You behave differently in the presence of different employees. You focus on different functions of the company (you and your body) when you meet with the COO than you do the CFO. But ultimately *you* are fairly consistent in your behavior. You think. Your parts and employees don't think. Your conscious mind doesn't spontaneously react. It considers, evaluates, and decides.

Your brain, and all of its parts, operates at near the speed of light when reacting to a stimulus that might bring you harm. Your *brain* is in reaction mode before the influencer ever shows up. Your *mind* (which analyzes) doesn't react; it responds. It resists. Your brain and all of its parts cause the body to behave, and then your mind justifies why your brain caused you to behave as it did just a half second ago. And that is the lag time between brain and mind.

I was playing catch with my son last night. When he throws quickly, there is no way my mind can possibly calculate where the ball is going and then end up there quick enough to catch the ball. My brain, however, enables me to catch the ball every time it is humanly possible to catch the ball.

I have a fairly good baseball player employee in my brain. He takes care of catching and throwing. If I (my conscious mind) stay out of the act of throwing the ball, my son won't have to move to catch it. The ball will end up within less than an arm's reach of his chest. If I think about where I'm throwing the ball, my probability for error and throwing the ball over his head or wide to his left is dramatically increased. My baseball player employee has thrown 200,000 balls in its existence. My conscious mind has thrown perhaps 10,000 balls over the course of my life. I don't have anywhere near the experience that my ballplayer employee does.

When you communicate with the person you are about to influence, you can trigger one of any number of parts of that person into the forefront, or you can trigger their mind to the forefront.

To simplify all of this, it's easier to think about all of these dynamic pieces as being parts of the brain and not the mind. But for the moment, let's just distinguish all the parts of the brain from the mind.

There is the rapid, reactive, fast action, decision-making lightning bolt of an unconscious brain; and there is a methodical, ponderous, conscious mind thinker. You and I refer to this as *you*.

Most of the time when you and the other person act, it is because of the automatic reactions and actions of the brain. Consciousness doesn't come into play as often as people would like to think.

The mind and brain don't do much "talking to each other," though they do share expenses for some of the space they rent in your brain.

Your Self Monitor Makes You Safe to Be With

Your Self Monitor helps you keep from screwing up too badly in most contexts, most of the time. It's very aware of how you smell, how you appear to others, how your nonverbal communication is being perceived, and how your communication is being received and processed.

You aren't born with a good Self Monitor. You have to shape it intentionally.

This is why the girl randomly grabbed the other girl's butt on the elevator, and the pinchee looked at her like she'd lost her mind. And that's kind of true. She lost her *mind*. She did what her *brain* moved her to do. Then the pincher had to make up an excuse with her conscious, thinking mind almost immediately after grabbing that blue-jean-covered piece of flesh.

Now you don't have to ask "What were you thinking?!" ever again. You know. You weren't thinking anything. The brain simply did what it wanted to before you could step in and stop it.

Become Aware of Selves, Yours and Others

Understanding this helps you in more ways than you can imagine. Mostly, this allows you to **be more influential and desirable to others**. The person who understands his Self has a much easier time **controlling his behavior**, his words, and not grabbing the cute girl's butt . . . at least not on the elevator.

The Awakening

There are two messages here:

1. Some of your Selves are valuable to the persuasion process. Some are not.
2. The person you are going to persuade has a number of interlocking Selves that may or may not be valuable to this conversation.

Recognize that when you are influencing someone you probably aren't immediately aware which of your employees is forward in the conversation. In other words, you don't know immediately which subroutine running in your brain is driving the conversation. That means you don't know the reactions that this part is likely to have in response to simple everyday phrases, words, and nonverbal communication the other person sends to you.

Self-awareness is a Keep-You-Alive Card.

Components of Self-Awareness

Being self-aware allows you to prepare for moments when you will be influencing others outside of your comfort zone.

Self-awareness can cover a lot of ground, but here are a few areas to consider:

The two of you are seated at the dinner table.

In front of you is the *TV Guide* page of the *USA Today Life* section and you've already circled *Big Bang Theory* for tonight at 7 p.m. By your left hand is your iPhone. It's on. It's been buzzing irritatingly. You haven't answered it, but you are waiting for one specific call from friends about going out on Friday night.

She has just put dinner on the table in between the two of you. She has no newspaper, no telephone, no items that show any interest other than having dinner with you.

You might as well just kiss and make up now.

The message of the newspaper with *Big Bang* circled, even though you're going to watch it together, is that it's important space on the table taking up 12 × 16 inches. You don't think a thing about it because you think it's about something you're going to do together. You're intentionally reminding yourself of something fun. You're just not really self-aware.

Meanwhile, she sees the cell phone as a message that every single being on planet earth at any random moment will become more important this evening than she is right now.

Self-awareness Strike 2. Obviously your thinking is that if you get the plans taken care of now you'll be able to watch *Big Bang* with her uninterrupted later.

Her: "How was your day today?"

Him: [Description of work project 1 today. Description of work project 2 today. Description of work project 3 today. Description of work project 4 today.]

Her: [Nods her head. She thinks, "I see how important I am. Probably 17th on his list of important people and things today."]

Him: "How was your day?"

Her: "Fine." [She thinks, "I'm not going to tell him how irritating and stressful dealing with the daycare lady is. She's moaning about needing to raise our fees and how she really should. I've now been up for 13 hours straight, traffic was bad on the way home, and I haven't done a single thing for myself all day except use the restroom."]

Him: "Well, that's good. I was thinking about inviting Keith and Mary over this weekend for dinner."

She eats silently and thinks, "You moron, you just don't get it. You're sitting here eating a great meal that took nearly an hour to make. I said 'Fine,' but you didn't probe, you didn't ask anything because you don't care, and now you want me to cook a dinner for the Johnsons, which you think is a nice idea, and it is for you, just not for me. I have to cook it, get the kids ready for bed, you just 'entertain them' while I'm busy in the kitchen."

Her: "Sure."

Him: "You wanna give them a ring after dinner?"

At this point he should invest in a bullet-proof vest. The earth-shattering noise alone would be enough to rip your heart out. You never saw any of it coming. You never even dreamed you were doing anything but being sociable. The ensuing argument is three hours and 12 minutes. . . . And you didn't even think to TiVo *Big Bang*. . . .

So what possibly could have gone wrong?

What did he need to be aware of that *you* also need to be aware of?

Observe your possessions.

Are you mirroring precisely what's on her side of the table?

You have a cellphone, it's turned on, you're waiting for a call, your intention is to take a call during dinner, you have an open newspaper, and you have a closed person.

After the brief response of "Fine," he could have asked a specific, such as "How did the meeting with X go today?" showing that he remembered something important and different about her day.

So, how do you prevent this disaster before it happens?

You ask, "Hey, do you want me to take a call from Nate and Tina when they call about dinner this evening, or do you want me to turn my phone off and take care of it tomorrow?"

Fold up the newspaper and put it out of sight.

Acknowledge and appreciate the food in front of you.

And lest you think the woman opposite is the completely innocent martyr, let's take a closer look:

1. The chef for the evening did not finish setting up the table, clearing up unwanted items like newspapers and cellphones, informing their owner where they could be found after dinner.

2. Her response of "Fine," will only elicit what it allows to be elicited. Our nonchef of the evening is not likely to say, "So specifically how was it not fine?" This only creates frustration for the chef.

You could go on and on and on with this, but you've already lived this yourself and you know how it ends. Being aware of everything in advance would have precluded everything that was about to cause the dam to burst.

The great lesson for the influencer here is that tomorrow when you go back out there to sell, to manage, work at the office, parent, and so on, you are going to have the exact same scenario with several other people. Your results will be similar and you will continue to be surprised. And without self-awareness, you will continue to fail.

6

Reactance Removed

Imagine you are taking a walk through an upscale neighborhood with a friend.

You are talking about all things persuasion, and your friend suggests an experiment. The framework is simple. You will walk up to randomly selected doors of upper-class homes (McMansions) in this neighborhood and **make an obviously valuable offer** that no one in their right mind could logically refuse.

How Can They Possibly Say No?

Your friend places a one-ounce gold coin in your hand. On the day of this experiment, its spot price is almost $1,800. Unlike other scientific experiments, your friend bets you $2,000 you can't sell the $1,800 gold eagle for $900 cash or check to an adult who opens the door to any of the next 10 houses.

It's a mostly sunny day: right around 70 degrees, just before noon on a Sunday in September.

You briefly pause, realizing the guy who opens the door is going to get a great deal. It's identical to exchanging $1,800 for $900. *Any idiot would do that.*

You will then get paid $2,000 and the transaction is complete.

Meanwhile, your friend will be out $2,900 ($2,000 to you and he'll get only $900 back from the transaction itself). But he'll live. He's made of money.

In the spirit of being a good guy, you accept the bet.

You walk up to the house. A 50-year-old doctor opens the door. The name isn't on the mailbox, but your experimenting friend lived in the neighborhood a few years ago and gave you the names of the people so you at least have that going for you as you walk up to the door.

"Hello Dr. Johnson, my name is William, and I have this gold coin that is worth $1,800 at today's spot price. I'd like you to have it for only $900."

"Thanks, my friend, but you have a good day. I'm busy."

"But, sir, this is a one-ounce eagle. Official U.S. Mint Issue. It's worth $1,800. You can check online and see. It's. . . ."

"That's okay. Thanks anyway. You have a good day."

The door is shut *and locked.*

What seemed obvious, what seemed so . . . ridiculously obvious has now become not so obvious.

Five of the remaining houses reveal open then closed doors. The result of all six was "No."

You have to give your friend $2,000, and he gets his $1,800 eagle back.

"You just learned **Lesson One of Persuasion 101**. And you learned it dirt cheap."

"I sure don't feel like I learned anything cheap. The guy should have snapped up the coin for $900. . . . It was a no-brainer. It's the same as offering him $1,800 for $900."

"You can stop freaking out now."

"It doesn't make any sense. They all should have said yes!"

"That's what everyone thinks. **The reality is you had almost no chance of making that trade.** You could have had 18 $100 bills, and they would *still* have closed the door politely in your face."

"But, it makes no sense."

Sweeten the Deal

"It makes all the sense in the world, which is why I made the wager in the first place. Look, I will bet you $1,000 that you will not be able to sell 10 $100 dollar bills for $500 to another random home owner in the community."

The friend pulls out his wallet and counts out 10 hundreds.

William takes the bet. He is out 2K, so this is an easy way to cut that in half.

The first door is randomly selected and he knocks. Different approach this time. The door opens.

"Hello sir, my name is William. My friend over there on the sidewalk, Kevin, has bet me $1,000 that you won't buy these 10 $100 bills for $500."

The man who opened the door saw Kevin, looked back at William, and promptly closed the door. Not even a word.

William has just lost another $1,000, which he didn't have.

Minutes later, Kevin gives all of William's money back (thereby almost certainly ensuring that his friend will not learn a thing from the experience).

"Okay, why would anyone not take $1,000 in exchange for $500? That's just crazy. These people are idiots."

Kevin shakes his head and smiles.

"These people are 100 percent normal. Perhaps 1 in 10 or 20 people will say yes to your offer."

The First Hurdle of Influencing Someone

The problem that William faced was in believing that **value** was the key criteria in persuasion and selling. And obviously, value is crucial in the long term. It just doesn't *make* sales. It does, however, keep customers forever, once you have them.

Value is *not* the key factor in selling or persuasion.

The first hurdle in influence is **overcoming reactance** (My understanding of reactance was crystallized and shaped by the work of Dr. Eric Knowles; see www.drknowles.com.)

Reactance is resistance to the influence.

Because most people attempting to influence others never think about the conversation that is going on in the head of the **other** person, reactance gets the best of the majority of "influence attempts."

The people opening the doors *did not want to be influenced*.

The failure to make the trade on William's part had nothing to do with his understanding that an ounce of gold was worth more than $900 by double. It had nothing to do with having the other person understand that the 10 hundred-dollar bills were worth more than 500 dollar bills.

The Value Equation is a secondary influencer and can only be used after successfully bypassing reactance.

Reactance = Show Stopper

The first thing you want to know is that the person who opened the door would happily take your ounce of gold in exchange for $900 if he was not reactant.

He'd do it all day and night.

When someone says they "aren't interested" in something prior to having analyzed the value of the actual experience, idea, product, or service, they are actually reactant to the *attempt* of unplanned and unprepared influence.

No Reactance = High Probability of Influential Success

Over the years, you and I have talked about the ridiculousness of scripts, the weaknesses of exact words, and parroting.

Once again, you can see that influence certainly can be enhanced by a few specific words, but most of the time, exact words don't cause influence.

You can't play a hand of poker with the pros until you are allowed to sit at the table. Saying "I've got it" or "I have Jacks" or any other sentence is not correlated to winning or losing a hand of poker.

Every excellent poker player understands that **words can be all but meaningless in influence**. They know speaking will usually cost them a lot of money in a pot where they know the other guy has a full house and he himself has four deuces.

The reason people have such a hard time with winning at poker is they can't shut up and understand the players. Instead they try to bluff. Or randomly try to say exactly what their hand is hoping for a future set-up. All these guys not only lose, they go broke.

When you study the truly great poker players, most have next to nothing to say while they are playing a hand that matters. There are definitely exceptions. Some of these players listen to music while they play to help filter out auditory messages from the other players. A few of the players attempt to engage other players into conversations during or between hands. Most know that remaining silent is their best opportunity to win.

That's a lesson to be remembered while influencing others.

A well-crafted question can go a long way in influence. Long-winded biographical sketches take you nowhere.

Poker players, however, lose their instinctive reactance early on. The good poker player, in the long run, can't be beat because he understands the players and how each of them thinks and makes their decisions. Great poker players are students of behavior stemming from emotion and thought, and other players' reactions to their exact **behavior** in any given and every given moment. They don't study exact words. They play no script. They play no foolish games.

Now you know what Reactance is. It's the sense—the reaction—that you will *lose freedom* of something if you move forward with something.

Is it too presumptuous to now generalize these situations across contexts?

Absolutely not.

William could have walked up to a girl in certain contexts, to a prospect in certain contexts, even to the men who opened then closed their doors—and *easily* have gotten a yes response.

What?

William could have made the **same** offer in **different contexts** and heard yes 99 percent of the time . . . perhaps 100 percent of the time. In fact he would have been swarmed and trampled by others looking for a chance to take advantage of his innocence.

It begins to feel like everything you learned in Sales 101 or Persuasion 101 was wrong.

Exactly.

Bypassing Reactance

Imagine that Dr. Johnson went to a coin shop owned by William. Or imagine that William was a well-known gold dealer and was approached by the first man. Or imagine that William accepted an office appointment with the man who refused the $1,000 cash in exchange for $500. Then what would have happened when William made the offer at the office? If the two men had been introduced by a respected mutual acquaintance, William would be out $500.

In all of these hypothetical cases, there will be little or no reactance. There is no resistance to the influence.

And there is no problem in getting $900 for a $1,800 ounce of gold.

If you want the opportunity to influence, you must bypass Reactance.

You've probably seen the TV show *Pawn Stars*.

Why is there absolutely no reactance on the part of the shop owners when they know they are going to be persuaded all day long, 24/7, 365?

They know that there is nothing to be reactant to! They've long gotten past reactance in *the context of the Pawn Shop*.

They know *every person will walk in wanting an unreasonable amount of money for their treasures*.

There's no reactance left. There is no fear of losing their personal freedom or freedom from anything.

It's all part of a logical process. Someone comes in the shop. Rick and Corey Harrison see the item, establish the value, offer between one-third and two-thirds the retail value. It's simple, basic math.

They set a number in their mind and never exceed that number. They have perfect self-regulation and self-discipline so that they don't make mistakes based on emotion.

Why Most People Fail to Influence

Because people are constantly trying to find the right words to say to someone, they ignore something that is 100 times bigger than the exact words: they ignore the **context**.

No one who teaches influence, selling, or marketing talks about **context**. Why?

It's not profitable to them.

The context is only profitable to you.

Teaching context is the same as teaching the poker player to understand human behavior in hundreds of situations. The guru knows that people are immensely lazy, and thus they tell their uneducated audience, "Don't pay attention to theory."

The only thing that happens at the pawn shop, at the poker table, at the guy's door with the gold coin in his hand, is theory. The guy with a script can't make money.

Specifically? The case of Dr. Johnson and the knocked door shows you the process of Reactance. And remember, while Reactance is triggered, you will **not** get the opportunity to attempt to influence.

Think about a scenario.

Dr. Johnson is snuggling with his girlfriend, watching the tube. They have no interest in being disturbed. The phone is off the hook.

The doorbell rings.

He thinks, "What the . . . ? I don't believe this. Another door-to-door? What do they want? Do they want free money, to sell me washer fluid, bid on the roof, bid on the driveway, donate to the gymnastics team, or want me to join their religion? They want something from me, and I never want anything from them."

The doorbell rings all the time in McMansion Territory. It's one of the maddening things about living there. Almost every single day someone wants something for nothing, or something for something else that is worth almost nothing.

You've thought the same thing in the same situation. Just comprehending the frame of mind of Dr. Johnson tells you this is a terrible strategy for "soliciting."

The doorbell rings again.

He thinks, "Whoever it is, he's not going away." He gets up and tightens his robe.

He walks across the house, preparing to not be a jerk, but also not to get sucked into any conversation, knowing that every second he stands at the door increases the probability seconds will turn to minutes. This is a neighborhood pest that you can't kill.

He sighs as he grabs the door handle and opens the door.

He's looking at a man with something shiny in his hand. At least it isn't a gun. He thinks, "I don't want to know. I don't care."

"Hello, Dr. Johnson . . ."

"Thanks, my friend, but you have a good day. I'm busy."

The guy mumbles something about $1,800 and $900 and gold, and Dr. Johnson, reiterates . . .

"That's okay. Thanks anyway. You have a good day."

He closes the door firmly, and he can now return to his previously scheduled moment, which, with luck, hasn't been destroyed.

"I will never answer the door again. Ever."

"Who was it, honey?" she asks, and he mentally promises himself one more time before trying to rekindle the ambience of the moment.

The Context Frames the Story

The rejection of the attempt to influence was predictable yesterday. And it will be tomorrow.

Does this mean Dr. Johnson will never under any circumstances answer the door or buy something or donate to a local cause?

Of course not. Contexts change all the time. However, in general, the reactance to just the doorbell ring is significant all by itself.

Opening the door to the stranger doubles the pain. Listening to the person babble quadruples the pain. Trying to be nice while watching some one's lips move seemingly without cessation, quintuples the pain.

There are very few pleasant moments attached to the unexpected doorbell ringing: 95 percent of the time it is painful and wrought with memories of being ripped off or being asked for something and getting no pleasure from the experience.

Reactance. The gut reaction to not wanting to lose freedom of choice or be manipulated.

You and I could spend an hour discussing strategy for getting past this specific reactance or something similar.

Instead, I'll give you a two-minute story so you can avoid the hour-long strategy session.

Bursting the Bubble of Resistance

When I was a kid, I was a Seventh Day Adventist, like my grandparents. In the summer, I'd travel with my grandparents. Before departing on a trip, I was slated to take $100 to the church office and buy 100 copies of the 80-page book *Steps to Christ*.

I had read the book a few times by the time I was 12 years old. We never did door knocking, but we "spread The Word," in other ways. It was something we were very proud to do, and we knew that the gesture of giving the small book as a gift would be politely accepted and occasionally spark a conversation. Gas station attendants and campground office staff were the typical recipients wherever we went.

Because I wasn't asking anything in return, including a conversation, it became quite easy to give people something, and if they wanted to chat, I was happy to do so, and every now and then did. I was 12 going on 25. The conversations were rare. "Thank you" was heard quite often, and more often than not, it ended at that. Outright rejection occurred at the hands of very few, generally by people who belonged to other Christian denominations. When that happened, it was no big deal. I was taught to feel sorry for them, and I did.

The notion of going up to someone and asking that person for anything was painful. The notion of **giving** someone something was pleasant and rather uplifting.

Very little reactance was observed when you gave someone a book and simply said, "Thank you and have a good day."

If you have to deal with certain reactance in a situation, you would generally want to give the reactant person **something of tangible valuable.**

Receiving something of value tends to stop reactant feelings from increasing.

As a rule, in any conversation, find a way to say, "Thank you" for something as early as possible.

"Thank you" ranks up there with "I was wrong" as words people like to hear, words that tend to set them at ease.

Briefly imagine how those gas station visits would have changed had I asked for a $1 donation for the church in return for the book. I would have grown up to feel very differently about First Contact. So would you or anyone else.

Reactance Is Essential

Reactance keeps people alive.

It is an important part of genetic wiring, and as you experience life, your brain finds environmental stimuli to hook into the reactant message that will be heard loud and clear by the body and consciousness.

When your freedom is threatened in some way, whether it is in regard to your time, possessions, or space, you feel reactance. *When you experience reactance to another, you are triggered to counter the force you perceive to be impinging on you.*

Reactant responses can change over time when your brain experiences new interpretations of data.

Meanwhile, on the other side of the coin, the answer is to give a gift or say "Thank you" for something.

It is important to remember that a gift is something that is appreciated or perceived to be valuable by another person. Someone could give you the gift of a beautiful dinner, but if you didn't like the food you wouldn't be thrilled with the gift, and certainly wouldn't be willing to offer your ear to listen to some kind of a proposal.

Understanding reactance creates a big shift in how you think about influencing others.

The most dramatic of those shifts is that you want to set the **appropriate context** for influence, or you can easily get shut out before you have an opportunity to communicate anything. In fact, that is what happens most of the time when you are in the wrong context.

Coffee with Kevin Hogan readers have written me for years with their questions about influence, and this specific problem is the most frustrating for me to respond to. They want any other solution than changing the context.

The best answer is more often than not to change the context. A person of influence always thinks context first, message second. *If you want to be excellent, design situations in that order.*

That means, if you really want to influence someone, make sure you carefully and deliberately create the setting. If you live in a strictly random world, you've put yourself behind from the beginning.

If you want to meet the girl, you have a mutual friend introduce you. A well-done introduction face to face reduces most of the reactance and resistance.

"Hey Kayla, this is Kevin. I was telling you about him last week. Now Kevin, you be quiet for just a minute. See, Kayla, be prepared for this guy because he won't tell you all of his secrets. He won't tell you about the charity work he did raising money for kids in Africa. He won't tell you about the fact that he leaped tall buildings in a single bound; oh, and he did okay as a writer too. And Kev, Kayla here is not just the hottest girl in town; she graduated from the U of K with honors. Her brain's as pretty as she is. And you should know that she has secrets too. She reads a lot of the authors you like, Greg Iles, Daniel Suarez, Suzanne Collins, Doug Kenrick, Geoff Miller, and well, I gotta run. You guys go have dinner on me. Kev, she likes red wine, the ones that cost a lot of money I imagine. See you guys later."

And it's over. He hit identification points for both of you. He had permission from both of you to set up the meeting.

This is how you best eliminate reactance.

Meetings are generally uncomfortable at first. But with a few threads of information, the conversation has easy places to go quickly. The discomfort will be gone in seconds. The reactance that would have been is now something that happens to other people.

"But Kevin, what happens if I see her over there and I don't have a friend to introduce me?"

You signal for the waiter. You tell him to bring a wine menu to her table. Ask the waiter to help them select the best wine they could hope for. You write on your business card, "Please stop over with your friend and say hello after you've enjoyed the wine." You ask the waiter to tell the girls that the wine is on your tab. He's to give the card to the girl and mention that you are rather taken by her and that, "he wants to meet you."

She will come over and say thank you in about 20 minutes. Possibly with her friend.

"I wanted to thank you for the . . . "

You stand up.

"Sit down. I insist." You signal for the waiter.

You speak first to the girl you are not interested in asking out. You ask her anything you like, except something that has to do with the friend you are interested in. Reactance is now eliminated. After a follow up, you can then make mutual eye contact with both of the girls and you have an ideal situation. No reactance. Almost no resistance.

If the girl is unimpressed, so be it. You were the classiest guy she's ever met. She either likes the brand or not. If they have to go somewhere, ask for her cell phone number and for her permission to text her tomorrow at this time. Text her once. That's it. Once. Win, lose, or draw, you've played the game well.

Other Ways to Overcome or Work Past Reactance

Overcoming reactance and resistance can also come from being prepared for FITD or DITF.

I've discussed FITD and DITF elsewhere, but these responses bear repeating. The lessons change lives across a broad spectrum of influence.

FITD = Foot in the Door

You've probably heard me tell this story. It illustrates overcoming reactance beautifully.

When I bought my first house, encyclopedias were in their final days as a species. It wasn't long after moving in that a guy came up to the house and said, "Welcome to the neighborhood, Mr. Hogan. I've stopped by to welcome you to the community and to give you a little gift."

He placed three books into my hands. A dictionary, a thesaurus, and Strunk and White's *Elements of Style and Grammar*. I laughed. Even then I had the awareness that before I died I'd want to learn grammar.

"My grammar is terrible."

Instead of going there, he said, "You're one of those smart math and science types."

Well, obviously.

And I smiled . . . and within 90 minutes I had spent $2,000 on a set of encyclopedias. I never regretted the purchase for one minute.

Hopefully this sounded familiar because it's precisely what happened in the restaurant in the scenario with the two girls.

The Foot in the Door Response is anything you can do . . . any small request that will keep the **Window of Opportunity** open for just a second longer to get the rest of the body through the window—to gain an opportunity to make a proposal.

The Foot in the Door Response could be:

- Giving someone a gift.
- Asking someone for a small favor, "I need a favor; do you have 20 seconds?"
- Saying thank you for something real: "I'm your new neighbor, and I wanted to say thanks for cutting that strip of lawn over there. I did recognize that and just wanted to stop by and let you know."

- Anything that gets the Window, the Door, their Mind—to stay open for just a few moments more.

DITF = Door in the Face

The Door in the Face Response is the other grand approach that is effective in 100,000 different contexts.

Here the strategy is almost the opposite. Here you want to ask for the moon, then back off fairly quickly to get to what you want to propose.

The famous university studies show something like this:

"Hi John, I'm with the Rehabilitate Juvenile Delinquent Center, and we'd like you to come down for three days to the prison and donate two or three days of your time teaching prisoners how to cook."

Waiting for the moon to sink in, you release the pain in about five seconds. "Or, if that wouldn't work, could we count on you for a donation of 10 dollars today?"

The Door in the Face Response is a psychological approach to working within reactance.

Literally experiencing the shutting door is fairly rare, though it does come close to that at times. But the pressure relief of the Ridiculous Request transformed to a very Reasonable Request is something that is remarkably effective in all of its manifestations.

And this is all in response to reactance.

Getting through or lowering reactance is absolutely necessary in order to influence others. Most, but not all, reactance reducing strategies take place long before a face-to-face experience takes place.

Here are 22 very effective ways you can do precisely that.

Advanced Intelligence Checklist

Twenty-two things you can do to avoid reactance:

1. Remove status symbol objects like rings, watches, pins that boast you won a big award or show your support of political causes.
2. When seating yourself at the table, always select a table at the back where your chair is facing out and they are looking only at you. You don't need

any visual competition from anything bad that might happen in the restaurant. If they are looking out and they see dishes breaking, observe bad behavior, or experience all kinds of other stimuli, that will trigger, no.

3. Arrive five to fifteen minutes early for every meeting. Learn your waiter's name so you can address him or her by name. That's always impressive to people. Find out where the restroom is. If you are the influencer and the other person is late and this is your first meeting, reframe that into an opportunity to revisit what questions you want to ask today.

4. Always research people or organizations in advance. Please don't tell them you did unless it becomes obviously advantageous, which is rare. If their Facebook page says they like *Big Bang Theory* and they mention another show they were watching, you can say "I like *Big Bang Theory*. Leonard and Sheldon just crack me up." You now have the sale. If they like Carrie Underwood, find out where Carrie Underwood is playing next. If you've got a $10,000 deal here, can you imagine what it would be like to hand over two concert tickets to the person you'll be meeting?

5. Check out their Twitter feed and find out what their rants are—what they complain about. If you find that, rapport just got a lot easier. As you look at social media, you may find out what someone's favorite reads are. You might be able to get an autographed copy. Fifty dollars for a big deal is definitely not a big deal.

6. Look on LinkedIn for where they went to school. If you have any link at all, maybe your football team played theirs and lost; that can make a good story.

7. Keep your back straight and avoid the temptation to lean into the conversation until the other person does. As soon as they reach for their napkin, reach for yours and put it on your lap regardless of what they do with theirs.

8. Be much more focused on asking questions than telling medium or long stories or reciting biographical information that causes other people's eyes to glaze over.

9. Ask questions like "How is it that you came to be so successful in business when so many other people fail?" or "Is there anything out there in marketing that's working right now?"

10. If you have obviously unique physical traits like a birthmark on your face, you'll notice the person look at it at some point. At that precise point you'll say, "Been driving me nuts for 30 years. I once looked in the mirror and said, 'Someday I gotta get that fixed.'" Let it be known that you are not nervous about personal attributes. You aren't afraid. Highlighting defects or weaknesses take the pressure off. They are off

the hook for hurting your feelings by staring. You can now talk about what it is you came to talk about.

11. Cultural differences. Don't be afraid to talk about cultural differences. More people screw up influence by avoiding culture or race than those who ask sharp questions about the same.

12. Don't outdress the other person. Dress to how you'll think they'll dress. The best way to handle it if you're inviting them to a business meeting is in the invitation. "If you don't wear a tie, I won't, either." What you don't want is to be there in a suit and tie, and they're in a polo shirt. If you get a complete mismatch—she's in cute jeans and a sparkly T-shirt and you're in a suit—highlight it early and laugh, take off the jacket and tie, and roll up the sleeves. Order a bottle of wine.

13. Avoid all talk of your medical issues or bodily functions. If you've been under the weather, use that phrase and leave it at that. You also don't want your value to be reduced by perceptions of weakness.

14. Never tell a joke. There are all downsides and few upsides. You'll laugh at her jokes and comments, but she'll find it hard to laugh at yours.

15. Vulgar language is tough because many people will use at least one word that wouldn't be allowed in church. Be careful not to match them, as they will see you as less than you are. Do not take the name of anyone's God in vain.

16. Never use the name of another human being unless it is completely necessary. You can say, "I met Madonna." But otherwise refer to people by job title or other description. You do not need to make your competitor's name stick out in their mind or give the impression you breach confidentiality.

17. When the other person criticizes someone as in, "My boss is such a jerk," feel free to elicit more about their boss, showing empathy, rather than instantly agreeing with their sentiment. You can say that the behavior would bug you if you experienced it. "I've met Bill and I've never seen him do that, but boy if I did, that would bug me."

18. Avoid any and all rude or high-handed behaviors toward servers, hosts, and other helpers. First, it's not necessary; they are there for a good reason. They also do not need unnecessary attention. They are not more important than your date.

19. Respond to their mode of communication with like communication. If they leave you a voicemail, don't text them back. Pick up the phone. Mirror their written greetings and farewells precisely. "Hi, Kevin." "Hi, Bill." "Good day, Kevin!" "Good day, Bill!"

20. Your speaking volume should be context dependent and wherever possible, speak at a quieter tone. If you have to take a phone call speak very quietly, but tell them in advance the important reason why you're taking it or simply turn your phone off.

21. Body language basic? Don't touch anything above shoulders or below your waist. Keep your hands close to your body. Don't knock the bottle of wine over with flailing arms.

22. Follow up? Make it clear at dinner or in the meeting precisely how you will follow up and then do exactly as you noted. "I'll give you a ring tomorrow at four and we'll talk through the details." Then do it.

7 | The Science of When

When you ask someone to say "yes" is often much more important than *how* you ask that person. It's more important than *what* you ask that person.

What *day of the week* matters more than you could guess.

What *hour of the day* you ask is mission-critical.

What *day of the month* could make all the difference in the world? In fact, there are more than a few periodic cycles that are crucial to understand.

Let's not pretend that when to ask is easy. It's not, or at least it hasn't been. Let's do this right and have you understand it clearly, so you never forget one of the big puzzle pieces that have been hidden under the couch of influence.

For a number of years I sold advertising. As time went on I would manage people who sold advertising, What was a day like for people who were selling advertising, whether that was me or someone I managed? We typically set 8 to 12 appointments a day, Monday through Thursday, and possibly a few on Friday or Saturday, all in person. A 55-hour week was pretty standard for salespeople.

For a few years after that I did fundraising for charities, also by appointment, asking business owners and managers for sponsorships and donations. I made maybe 10 appointments per day. Interwoven in these experiences were a couple of stints as a telemarketing sales manager and a fundraising manager for a large national foundation.

I always assumed my experiences were unique to me and wouldn't be similar to other people's experiences. Most people believe similar notions. People feel comfortable with the idea that their experiences are unique.

The experience of one person is usually enough to set up experiments and do research to test what is learned from that person's experience. In other words, does the experience of Kevin Hogan generalize to other situations with different people involved? I never really knew until I took my experiences to companies where I would manage fundraising or sales teams.

Through thousands of appointments for which I was religious in my bookkeeping, I made some interesting revelations.

When *matters more than* ***how***.

When selling advertising, two trends emerged that seemingly had nothing to do with me or the presentation I used. (Meetings with owners and managers took place Monday through Friday.)

I found that I sold almost half of my weekly advertising on Monday. I also sold the highest percentage of appointments kept on Monday. If you had asked me a decade ago, I'd have remembered precisely what the results were. Let's call it 40 percent. When I trained people I would do everything in my power as a manager to get salespeople to see owners early in the week when possible. I worked long 10- to 12-hour days if possible, early each week. These results were similar in both fundraising and in selling.

For over five years I sold the majority on my morning appointments. Appointments right before lunchtime tended to be not as impressive. My 2:00 p.m. appointments were exceptional, and after that I sold a thin minority of prospects the balance of the day. I can still remember my Daytimer being asterisked heavily on the top of the day and relatively starless at the bottom of the day. And 4:00, 5:00, and 6:00 p.m. appointments were miserable all week long.

When I was a phone room manager, we kept pinpoint accurate records of tens of thousands of calls, sales made for the sales company and donations for the nonprofits. Hours were 3:00 to 9:00 p.m. for some organizations I worked with, and 4:00 to 9:00 p.m. for others, and in all cases we were calling homeowners.

The afternoon appointments, we pondered, should do the best, as the homeowner would have fewer distractions. After dinner we figured would do worse. That was not the case selling coupon books. That was not the case selling people to visit a timeshare resort. That was not the case asking for donations or block workers.

In reality, in all cases, the *opposite* was the fact.

Across this spectrum we always found the same thing. On a percentage basis we did relatively poorly from 3:00 to 5:00 p.m. This was true regardless of who was calling: me, my star reps, or the people we were hiring almost off the streets. The dinner hour of 5:30 to 6:30 p.m. was typically decent in results and then the rest of the evening we were brilliant. In the 2½ hours from 6:30 to 9:00 p.m. we made more money per person reached by phone than in the first half of the evening, by over 2:1.

In telemarketing, whether for charity or selling, or getting people to go to a timesharing event, statistical records were everything.

I remember at one resort the owners were expected at dinnertime. We had a crummy afternoon, which was no surprise. This one particular day, which was around Christmas, they were blessedly late and as they arrived around 7:30 p.m. we were handing in slips like we were printing them from the Federal Reserve.

I was never able to explain these bizarre results.

It simply made no sense to me that from 7:00 to 9:00 p.m. you'd sell two or three times as many people answering the phone as you would from 3:00 to 5:30 p.m. For years whether making my own calls or training this simply was the case.

It took me quite some time before I finally pieced together a prediction and then came across what I believe are the answers.

Across nonprofit and aggressively for-profit organizations, across selling and fundraising functions, whether I was selling advertising, coupon books, or timesharing, it was universally true that Monday and Tuesday generated the highest per capita sales. Wednesday and Thursday were a waste of time. There were a few blips, like Friday night for telemarketing fundraising or for-profit was **excellent**.

Early in the morning was typically far superior to late morning. After lunch was generally quite good, but late afternoon was universally poor in person (and as mentioned above, on the phone as well).

Three Factors That Mattered When

Each year that passed my skills in getting to yes increased significantly. I remember many, many, many days when I would have five or six consecutive successes early in a day and then wonder if I would hear yes all day. Often my results would not hold for the final three to six appointments. But many, many times I was perfect through the first five or six.

I don't believe the afternoon was ever as fruitful.

You Aren't Going to Hear Yes When This Gets in the Way

I'm assuming you don't sell for a living, so I'm going to use a different context to let you see how this works.

Self-regulation is something like self-control.

Self-control is the ability to control what your Self actually does. It has nothing to do with what you think or how you feel but what you and everyone else actually sees your Self do.

Do you scream at the kids in the heat of the moment, or not?

Do you steal the stuff you forgot to put on the conveyor belt at the grocery store, or not?

Do you get up in the morning and get right on to the most important projects of the day, or not?

Do you hit the child who bullied your child or do you call the parents, the police, or the principal?

Do you eat the chocolate chip cookies when you shouldn't, or not?

Do you take care of the projects around the house or do they sit and wait for another day?

People can regulate or control their behavior with differing degrees of success. Everyone is internally driven to impulsive action. Self-regulation is the gasoline that keeps reaction to impulse desires squelched.

You and I generally begin our day with close to a "full tank" of Self-Regulation "Units" (SRUs). Some people run out of those units pretty fast in the day and live most of the day yielding to impulses to misbehave in any number of ways. Other people get better mileage per gallon of self-regulation and can last further into the day.

Self-regulation, for most people, will run out on most days. What happens in practice is that people tend to self-regulate one area of their lives at the expense of others. You'll see why that happens in a minute.

The SRUs allow you and me to control our behavior so that we can focus on and attain our desires. Self-regulation is critical to influence because once you are out of units for the day you probably can't be influenced to do anything but the most impulsive of behaviors. If you are an influencer, you want other people to be **high** in Self-Regulation Units so they can control their reactance to you, giving you a chance to cause a yes response.

Talking to people who are out of units for the day is like talking to loose cannons. There are no yeses to be heard when volatility enters into the picture, as you are about to discover.

Each time we exercise or utilize self-control, we burn up SRUs.

You only have so much self-control at your disposal each day. Sometimes you can get some Self-regulation units back through one of two behaviors, but don't count on that when self-regulation runs out.

Perhaps You Wake Up with 100 SRUs

Your kids are acting like normal kids this morning and, instead of killing them, you decide to sustain your wrath and allow them to live. That cost you five Self-Regulation Units. You used self-restraint. You're down to 95.

The spouse said something incredibly stupid, and you chose not to point out their temporarily low IQ and social skills. That took eight SRUs. Why? Because it took a **lot more** restraint *not to lay it on the line* with someone over 21, than someone under 13. You expect more from a 40-year-old. It takes more restraint when your expectation is further to the right to keep you from spouting off at them.

Now it's almost time to head to the office, and you are down to 88 SRUs. Twelve down and you haven't gotten out the door yet. Self-egulation Units get burned up pretty quickly.

Imagine you've been reading some self-help books lately, and you really want to make some life changes. Lots of new goals and even a handy dandy time management planner.

Where Do You Find Real Self-Help?

Unfortunately, people don't know the myriad reasons why they fail, and the "self-help" books often make it all sound so easy. In fact, people can religiously adhere to the prescriptions in the books and typically have absolutely nothing positive come from their efforts. And, certainly, that is typically true over the long term.

Life *can be* a lot easier than it currently is but only if you can understand what is really at work.

The concept of SRUs is crucial to success and failure. Most people who succeed have only a **hint** as to **why** they "got lucky." Or worse, they mis-attribute the causes of success, and then you go modeling them and nothing works . . .

. . . you were down to 88.

A good night's sleep will reset you back to close to 100, tomorrow, but every time you have to exercise self-restraint or intentionally control your behavior, you use up SRUs today.

As soon as you use your daily supply, you are out.

How fast or slowly can 88 units run out? And *then* what happens?

The drive to work—you get cut off. You yell at the other driver (no self-regulation) and therefore no units are used up. "Bad behavior" can pay off!

Then it happens again five minutes later, but this time, you choose not to have road rage. You don't honk the horn and you don't scream. And you use four units.

84. You look at the doughnuts you bought at Dunkin Donuts. (No units used up.)

You could eat them. No SRUs would be used up if that is the case.

You decide to be healthier and not eat them. You'll save them for the kids tonight. Your self-control just cost you six units.

78. Now you get to the office and throw the donuts into the trash on the way in (five more units) to the office.

Had you eaten one of the doughnuts you'd have actually **added** SRUs back into the brain and body. One doughnut could perhaps have bought you four to seven units. Sugar is one of the few things that actu-ally boosts self-regulation. Your decision cost you precious units but saved your arteries.

73. You get to the desk and there is an envelope indicating you have to fire someone. (No units used up.)

You fire the person. (No units used up.)

You control and compose your Self . . . choosing carefully *not* to yell at your boss who made you do the firing and you are disgusted with her request to the point where you could smack her a good one (10 SRUs used up).

63. Customers call with complaints this morning, and you stay cool under the gun several times before noon. You control your words, your temper, your attitude, and at no point do you lose it. You keep your thoughts inside of your brain and out of your mouth (19 units evaporate).

Lunch comes and everyone is heading to the nice restaurant across the street. Coworkers are all enjoying drinks, but you refuse the alcohol so you can keep your tongue and maintain control today. Alcohol reduces inhibition. You see the fantastically tasty food options, refuse them all, opting for salad and an iced tea (14 units used). No glucose pretty much means no SRUs replenished. Dieting has benefits, just not for building SRUs.

30. Your co-workers rib you for your prudish choices and you choose not to return the volley (four units used up).

26. You get back to work and open the mail on the desk. You see that the IRS has chosen to audit you (zero units used up).

You have done nothing wrong, but they want $30,000 in extra taxes for some mumbo jumbo reason (still zero units used up). You are angry (still zero units used up). You throw the letter and all the mail against the wall (still zero units used). Your rage at this ongoing injustice grows, and you choose not to call them and tell them to go jump and stay jumped (12 units used up).

14. You open the desk drawer and grab a stash of M&Ms and munch away. (Zero units used and in fact you get two bonus units pumped into the gas tank!)

16. An employee comes in whining that they need the rest of the day off to go take care of a sick spouse at home. You roll your eyes. You think of how unnecessary this is, but choose not to tell her off (six units used up) and send her on her way.

10. The rest of the day is engaged in open, straightforward debate over corporate policy. (Zero units used.)

The drive home is uneventful.

You are exhausted and when you get home people expect you to cook. Instead of telling people to cook for themselves, you decide to just let it slide and start cooking. You make a nice dinner with a big fruit salad that by itself could give you several units but you never get to it (five units used).

5. The spouse returns from her day and she is in a good mood (zero units); it drives you nuts that their day was good and yours was bad (zero units), but you choose not to complain about your day or point out how wimpy their job is (five units used).

SRU Count . . .

Everyone sits down for dinner and the kids start spouting off about how they are sick of their teachers and the new school rules relating to dress and behavior.

You cut like a knife into the conversation. "In the real world you'll be praying for days like that. **Big deal!** Grow up! Now shut the +#!@ up and pass the damn vegetables."

The place goes silent.

You are an obvious psychopath ... mentally disturbed ... deranged ... and when you pull out the self-help books or whatever . . . there are no more self-control units available for your behavior.

You eat pasta like a horse. You down food that tastes good. You slam the door. You have no control of your behaviors. You simply do what you feel like doing, and it actually "feels cathartic" to do so.

No one wants to talk to you and you don't care. You just want peace.

You might get one or two units from the downed food. Maybe.

The idea of doing anything other than watch a TV show is laughable. There will be no self-improvement. You want to have a drink, relax, and just let it all hang out.

Work on a part-time business from home?! Not a chance. You've had it.

Tomorrow you will pick up the pieces.

But . . . until then it's popcorn and beer, baby. The popcorn could possibly bump you up a few units. The beer might briefly give you a unit, but you'll lose it when it reduces inhibition in 15 minutes.

The answer?

For today, know that **one change will help enormously**. The amount of SRUs you get every day is not absolutely fixed, but it is not easy to change the size of the gas tank on your car.

Also know that SRU's are given more generously to those who sleep well and to those who develop toughness in their use of self-regulation. What knocks off 10 SRUs today might only knock off 8 a year from now.

The Influencer **must** have Self-Regulation Units when influencing others, or they won't be able to influence others.

The other person **must** have Self-Regulation Units to be open to influence.

But on this day, you just ran out. Your ability to influence is shot. Anyone asking you for anything aside from being scorned and beaten will hear "No."

If you need to be influential, *you need to work on those projects, meetings, contacts that will give you the future you want, first each day.* You will not have the SRUs to fight an empty gas tank for long.

That said, this doesn't mean you have to be a "day person" instead of a "night person." One great advantage of being a night owl is the ability to get stuff done **because** no one else is around to e-mail you, to ask you for favors, to go to the doctor, to interact. You get a chance to get things done without the distractions and disturbances of the day.

Specifically, with no distractions at 1:00 a.m., you can work without the requirement of self-regulation. There is no one to upset you, bother you, interrupt you, or cut you off in traffic. You can get stuff done on **zero** Self-Regulation Units when there is no additional requirement for self-control.

If the work you are doing at night is creative and fun, fascinating and exciting, it requires **no SRUs**.

That said, building a website, writing a program, unless fun, are best done at the crack of dawn or long before lunch!

Each sales call I ever had was an interaction of two people's Self-Regulation Units. *Every situation where you will influence someone, or not, is an interaction of **two** people, both of whom require SRUs.*

Imagine trying to influence the lady at the dinner table in the scenario I mentioned earlier. She'd have had someone's head on a platter.

*You don't want to try to try to be persuasive when someone is **low** on Self-Regulation Units.* Two factors interact.

1. *You are at your worst as far as presenting your best self.*
2. *You are sitting opposite or on the phone with someone who is at her worst.*

With only a couple of exceptions as the day goes on, your Self-Regulation Units are drained hour by hour. As they are lowered, or when they are gone, so is your emotional intelligence. The answer more often than not will simply be no!

You want to communicate with someone when they are *high* in Self-Regulation Units. The more units they have to deal with you and your presentation, suggestion, idea, the better chance you have of them saying yes.

The science matches the years of sales and fundraising experience. It mirrors hundreds of thousands of tracked phone calls, fundraising presentations, and sales requests by several hundred different people.

You might be thinking, "But don't I want to see someone when their self-discipline is low so they are more likely to buy from me?"

There are *some* things that people buy and do that are more likely to occur when self-regulation is low.

They are more likely to break their diet.

They are more likely to grab a cigarette.

They are more likely to throw caution to the wind.

Yes. They will be more likely to go to McDonald's, to the bar, or to the club. They will buy a Reese's when in the checkout lane at Target.

But in general they are much more reactant and that means no to your wonderful products and services. They do not want to listen to you when they are out of SRUs. They want ice cream.

But this still doesn't explain why Monday was far and away the best sales day in the week for all businesses. It doesn't explain why Friday was the worst *except* Friday night for telemarketing.

With the benefit of hindsight, a lot of research, and mental modeling, I believe I have an answer.

People think in terms of time periods:

Hours
Days
Weeks
Months
Years
Decades

Time markers are both psychological and real in nature.

In the United States, in the twenty-first century, most people who work do so Monday through Friday. They take the weekend off. The hours they work in the course of the day probably come close to 8:00 to 5:00 p.m., unless they are in retail, of course.

More people die on Monday morning than any other day of the week. People, like Garfield the cat, tend to "hate Mondays." They are more likely to take Monday off than any other day in the week.

On the flip side, their body is coming off of perhaps two days of rest. They have restored their Self-Regulation Units back to 100. I believe that Monday morning for most people is the time when people are at their maximum number of Self-Regulation Units in the course of a week.

This is true for the first day of a month.

For years stock traders have known that if you buy on the close of the last trading day of the month and sell on the close of the first trading day of the month, you are going to make a lot of money over the long run.

The point is that time frames are not only important but because they are so culturally and seasonally specific, we can predict how people will respond and when people will respond favorably to whatever it is you sell.

If you own a bar and want people to drink a lot, Monday morning is when people have the most Self-Regulation Units and Friday before lunch is probably the lowest level. If you own a bar there is no point to being open Monday morning.

Perhaps you wake up Monday morning with (hypothetically) 100 SRUs. If that is the case then you wake up Tuesday with about 95. Wednesday? 90. Thursday with 80, Friday with 50. And Friday at about 5:00 p.m., your SRUs take a brief spike UP to 40 or 50 where most days around 5:00 p.m. you're probably closer to 10 or 15, if that. I believe this is because people are excited and invigorated that it is the weekend.

The Friday night bump in sales that we had telemarketing is likely part of that kind of euphoria that briefly restores 40 points of Self-Regulation Units ever so briefly . . . until it is time to go out and you have permission to eradicate *all* Self-Regulation Units.

And you want to influence the person when they are out of SRUs? You want to perhaps sell them life insurance? A car? A dog? A timeshare?

Of course not.

If you or what you have to sell, promote, or suggest is not something the person impulsively resists that causes self-regulation to drain, you probably don't want to try to sell it when the person is out of SRUs.

Eventually all companies I worked with experienced almost identical experiences. Thus we were able to make changes.

For example, setting appointments on Friday when the caller and the listener both have 10 SRUs left is good strategy.

But asking to *see* someone on Friday for an appointment is generally fiscal suicide.

Setting your best appointments, those that have the greatest reward and the greatest loss if you lose them, should go Monday morning but not at 11:15 a.m. If you can't get early morning, you shoot for Tuesday morning. If that doesn't work, you go for Monday 2:00 p.m. but no later. Next would be Wednesday morning.

What would they prefer?

Most people would rather meet, have an appointment, or get asked out when they aren't all stressed and freaked out. As a rule, assume people would like to say yes to you. That assumption then can stand on this premise:

You want good stuff to happen to this person. You want them to experience great things around you, with you, in life.

Therefore you would only really ask for anything when they are comfortable, at ease, at their best, and experiencing a state of mind where seeing you and talking to you is experienced as a benefit to them.

If you want to ask the girl out, you want to think about how she will perceive your offer. Be honest with yourself:

Are you the candy in the checkout line?

Ask her late at night.

Are you the "iffy" guy?

Catch her early in the week and early in the day.

Understanding who you are in the mind of the person you're asking to see is obviously more important than any line you could say in the proposal or suggestion.

Remember: ask the judge at 9:00 a.m. if you can go free and he'll say yes.

Ask the judge at 11:30 a.m. or 4:00 p.m. and he'll say no.

If you understand the science behind the layout of a grocery store, you will forever lock the concept of Self-Regulation Units into your brain.

When you go grocery shopping, you know you should come home with lettuce, carrots, apples, blueberries, whole-grain bread, and all that is good and healthy.

And you know that you should probably cut back on candy bars, ice cream, candy, sugared drinks, and snacks.

The grocery store management knows you struggle with this and therefore organizes the store in a profitable way.

When you enter the store you are relatively high on Self-Regulation Units. You know your mission as it is each week (and typically fail): to eat healthy.

You come to the healthy foods first. That means it requires no power of will to say no. Instead these are easy "Yes, of course" decisions. Each decision takes a few SRUs away but only a few for each one.

As you move like the mouse in the maze through the store, you find neutral decisions in the middle. Things like paper plates or cups.

At the far end is the ice cream and frozen pizzas, and once you are in line you face the decision to add Reese's, Snickers, French Silk Pie, and chocolate ice cream to your cart.

And you tend to do so particularly if you have loaded up with other stuff. The taller the pile in your cart, the more SRUs you probably have used en route to the register.

By the time you've spent your hour of making 75 decisions, you are out of SRUs.

You grab a pie, ice cream, Reese's, and Snickers. You deserve it after all. You have no more power to say no for any reason. It's all going on a credit card anyway.

The more decisions you make before you hit the sugar and fat, the better for the store's profits.

Once Self-Regulation Units are used up, then anything goes. Caution is thrown to the wind. Self-control is gone.

Once Self-Regulation Units are used up, people say, "Screw it. I don't care. I'm tired. I want to get out of here."

Catch people when their SRUs are still holding them up.

52 Techniques

I'm one of those people who, when I run into someone I've worked with somewhere at some point in the past, they say, "Kevin, it's so good to see you!"

That's what you want for the rest of your life. If at any time you feel like you wouldn't sell your product to your mom, your dad, your sister, or the next-door neighbor, then don't sell it to anyone else. Instead, tell a sales manager at a company whose products you like that you will be his next star salesperson. Not everyone should buy from you, not every girl should say yes to you. Your children should not always comply. And finally there are times when you need to be influenced by others.

The following techniques sometimes include dialogue that might sometimes seem a bit stilted because the situations are decontextualized. If you read the following sentences, you'll quickly get the idea of what you want to sound like (and what you don't want to sound like) when communicating with people you need to influence. Just think about how the messages feel to you and be very aware of how you want others to perceive you. There aren't necessarily right and wrong answers here, but most people I know who communicate in the "A" way don't seem to do as well as the folks who communicate in the "B" way!

Read and compare the feel of the following pairs of sentences:

A. "My, you look lovely today. You really brighten up a room."
B. "Hey, you look good."

A. "My goodness, that's a beautiful painting. It really adds to the ambience of the room."
B. "Where did you get that cool painting?"

A. "Your hair looks absolutely fabulous like that."
B. "I like your hair like that. Looks good."

A. "I really love what your company has done in the community. You must be really proud of all your employees and all the hard work and time spent volunteering to help the needy people in the community."
B. "What you guys are doing here is making a big difference."

It's really easy to take any of the 52 techniques you're about to learn and make them sound so goofy or cheesy that the other person could do nothing but laugh and say . . . "No."

If what you're selling requires a crowbar in a person's brain to open a door, you're selling the wrong product. If someone is so offensive that they have to beat somebody over the head to get them to say "Yes," they need to learn how to be real people.

Never sell a product you don't like. Ever. Never portray yourself in a way you are not going to behave for the rest of your life.

Here is the difference between hard-sell persuasion and elegant influence: The latter is like having people follow the scent of perfume, rather than dragging them along because you have "something fantastic" to show them.

The person who wants to be with you, as a rule, isn't reactant to you.

She just wants to make good decisions, and that is precisely what she should be doing.

Unfortunately people are going to make decisions based on their history of how they process information. Most people process information with subjective, inaccurate, and erroneous ideas that they use to generate decisions. Then they justify them with facts that match what they have already decided.

I like to point out thinking processes to people in the moment because it makes them aware that they are using potentially faulty circuitry from the past, when they might prefer to do something that makes more sense.

A sampling of factors people commonly use in decision making:

- **People assume** that when they decide on something and it turns out well, that **they made a good decision**, when it easily could have been attributed to chance (luck).
- **People tend to overemphasize** the importance of **pain** by about 2.5:1 in decision making. (People may not need to feel great, but they don't want to hurt at all).
- **People rationalize** their emotional **decisions** instead of making rational decisions.
- **People make** their **decisions impulsively**, and then stand by their impulse as if the decision was made rationally.
- **People make** their **decisions** based upon **their experience** and not the experience of the masses.
- **People make decisions** based upon the **socioenvironmental frames** or context they put the decisions into (a woman going to Planned Parenthood for counseling will get different advice than the woman going to her conservative pastor).
- **People** tend to **make decisions on their own** instead of seeking the counsel of numerous others who can give additional perspectives.
- **People are unaware** as to **how** the influence of specific **questions** changes their minds unconsciously. ("Are you sick of driving that old junker?" versus "Are you thinking of driving a new car?")
- **People tend to avoid** what they perceive as **risky**.
- **People tend to decide on "the sure thing"** even when it doesn't make real sense to do so. (They will take a sure $50 instead of a 50/50 chance at $125).
- **People tend to make decisions without** a solid **understanding of** the real-life likelihood of events (read this as mathematics, statistics, and probability).

Read and study the list of common rules of thumb that people use in making decisions. Incorporate this understanding into your approach with the other person. Not everyone needs to be told they are making decisions based on past programming. Some will find that arrogant or jarring. I know a lot of persuaders who like to take advantage of the programming and just flow their message through the circuitry that way.

Ultimately, either approach is fine. It's a personal preference. All of the techniques that follow in this section occur in an almost random context. I've tried to mix them up by matching sales, marketing, managing, dating, and so forth. You, of course, will **not** be showing up in a random context any time soon. You will create contexts that are optimal for you to communicate your message. Nothing is going to be more effective in gaining compliance.

All techniques are used in a context and the success of a technique is dependent on that context; in certain contexts only a few different kinds of technique can be used. Meanwhile other techniques are helpful in a wide variety of contexts.

It's not reasonable to simply read 52 techniques and then think, "Got it." Don't do that. Feel free to preview them all today, but let's do something that will actually make a difference in the long term.

Write a technique down, put it on your computer or in your wallet, and use it this week. Use another technique next week. Learn them until you don't need to remember them because they are part of your unconscious processing with other people.

1 | Preempting the Neon Sign

This book began by explaining the significant influence that your absolute and certain expectations have on the behavior of others.

Your expectations of someone literally change how they perform. If you are the right person, your expectations can matter more than you would have guessed before reading this book. You saw how 51 women were created in the image of the photograph the man held in his hand. You saw randomly assigned Israeli soldiers' Command Potential completely changed by one word inked in a manila folder.

When you walk into an office, a home, a restaurant, or a playground you have certain expectations of what's likely to happen in that environment. Meanwhile, as you're walking in the door, others see you and have expectations of how you're going to affect them.

That expectation is reactance. It arrived long before you did. Your early task is to change their expectations, not just about you, but about the suspicion that they are about to be manipulated by you.

Using questions early in a conversation allows the person to feel that you are yielding control of the situation and conversation so that they can have the floor.

You're at a prestigious private school in the admissions process. You finally meet the president of the school in his impressive office. You say, "So we're here to talk about putting my son into your school. I understand you have very high criteria for acceptance; can you tell me about that?"

Instead of reciting your biography, your credentials, your status in the community, the president of the school is looking at you while he explains to you who their ideal candidates and families are. All of his communication is directed to you, and all of his feelings about criteria are projected onto you. You don't have to sell yourself; you simply have to ask the right questions.

After the president of the school tells you his criteria, you simply ask, "So what do you want to see in our family and our son? Is there anything else?" Your lack of hesitation, the fact that you showed no fear, desperation, or concern about whether you would be accepted, is precisely what the president of the school *did not* expect to see. His expectations have been changed.

You're now sitting across the table from the girl. You've listened to her concerns about her past relationships; you have nothing that you need to tell her about yourself to set her mind at ease. You simply ask, "What would you like to see in a good relationship?"

If you were at the office with your manager and you wanted approval for a budget increase to work on a marketing project, you don't try to convince the boss how amazing and cool your idea is. You simply ask him what results he would expect to see when the marketing project is complete, and then tell him how much extra money you need allocated to achieve that.

The expectation that they all had about you was that you were going to try to put a big neon sign out there saying how wonderful you are. Instead, you asked specifically what their expectations of this specific situation were, and silently implied that that's exactly what they would get.

2 | Is Less More?

The next three techniques are captured from a massive marketing study carried out by a lender of money in South Africa in 2005.[1]

Unlike most studies that are done on a college campus with adult students, this study was done with 51,000 South African recipients of a direct mail piece soliciting loans to customers who had borrowed money from the lender in the past couple of years.

The goal of the study was to find out *what caused people to respond to the direct mail marketing and what didn't.*

Would lower or higher interest rates make a difference? What about differences that had nothing to do with the borrowing of money?

The direct mail pieces sent out were subdivided in several ways, which only could have been done in such a large magnitude experiment like this one.

- They tested for **different interest rates**, ranging from 3.25 to 11.75 percent per month.
- They **compared their interest rates to competitor rates** that were higher and stated so in different ways in tables.
- They tested for the **inclusion of three different tables** that showed various combinations of repayment terms. The third table was a small table with one loan size, one loan term, one monthly repayment, and one interest rate.
- They tested for **photos** and **similarity of last name of letter author** . . . of lender employees who were sending the letter, and that person's **race and gender** were manipulated depending on the race and gender

[1] M. Bertrand, D. Karlan, S. Mullainathan, E. Shafir, and J. Zinman, "What's Psychology Worth? A Field Experiment in the Consumer Credit Market" (Yale University Economic Growth Center Discussion Paper No. 918, July 2005).

of the recipient of the letter (guessed by the names of the people). Then 10,000 pieces were sent with no photo as a control for this variable.

- The offer **frame** was tested for several things, including the examples below:
  a. The **positive/negative** frame: "If you borrow elsewhere (from us), you will pay R100 Rand more (less) each month on a four-month loan."
  b. The **monthly saving/total saving** frame: "If you borrow from us, you will pay R100 (R400) Rand less each month (in total) on a four-month loan."
  c. The **percentage points/total percent** frame: "If you borrow from us, your interest rate will be 4.00 percent lower!" versus "If you borrow from us, you will pay 32 percent less each month on a four-month loan."

Now that you know what kinds of things they were looking at, would you like to know what influenced people to take a letter to the lender and get a loan?

- To begin with, the letters **with a small table** indicating one loan amount, one term, one monthly repayment amount, and one interest rate, **returned better** than those letters with bigger tables that included, say, four possible loan amounts and four possible repayment options . . . *the small table was most successful.*

The authors calculated that the table size and information included was so important that the interest rate offered would have needed to be 2.3 percent lower per month for the letters using the big tables to generate customers bringing the letter to the lender's office for a loan.

Think about that: the amount of information in the table had the same value in customer response as a 2.3 percent lower interest rate . . . !

Generally speaking, the more information your client considers and the more they evaluate, the more information you need to give them. The less information they want, the more likely they will say no if you go into great detail.

As far as how much information to give someone, here is a good rule of thumb:

The more expertise the other person has in a given area, the more features (not benefits) that person needs information about to make a decision. They are going to match your message to what they already have stored in their memory and mind. If you come across as not knowing the actual working details of whatever your idea or proposal is, you lose. If you have quality information, you engage the client and optimize your chances of making the sale.

When a person is not an expert in a certain area, less information is generally more likely to be processed more quickly and favorably. And because in this case less is better, you want that message to be very different. You want to share benefits, not features, with this client. When the client is not an expert, peripheral cues become crucial.

3 | Practice Deframing

The next discovery in the 2005 South Africa study was which "offer frame" results were seen to be the most effective.[1]

The study tested the offer frame in a number of ways:

- The **positive/negative** frame: "If you borrow elsewhere (from us), you will pay R100 Rand more (less) each month on a four-month loan."
- The **monthly saving/total saving** frame: "If you borrow from us, you will pay R100 (R400) Rand less each month (in total) on a four-month loan."
- The **percentage points/total percent** frame: "If you borrow from us, your interest rate will be 4.00 percent lower!" versus "If you borrow from us, you will pay 32 percent less each month on a four-month loan."

Survey says?

By far, the most profitable frame was the **loss** frame.

Additionally, **descriptions in terms of actual money were much more effective** than percent or interest rates.

As a technique, here's what you need to know:

Create a word picture that creates a moderate amount of tension if the person doesn't connect with you or if a client doesn't do business with your company. In other words, in a selling situation, what will the client **lose** if they do **not** do business with you?

People fear loss and think about it all the time. But this is different than random considerations. You are intentionally inducing the process of deframing.

---

[1] M. Bertrand, D. Karlan, S. Mullainathan, E. Shafir, and J. Zinman, "What's Psychology Worth? A Field Experiment in the Consumer Credit Market" (Yale University Economic Growth Center Discussion Paper No. 918, July 2005).

Deframing is more effective in some contexts than others. Consider what is potentially going to be lost, and compare it to the cost of being with you or doing business with you.

Loss aversion is more pronounced for safety than money. People will do more to protect themselves than their money. Loss aversion is more pronounced for income than leisure. (Losing a chance to travel isn't as powerful as losing income.)

Determine what people **lose** if they don't do business with you and artfully develop word pictures that clarify the hurt they might experience if they don't.

"For every person who dies this year in the United States, **seven** will become disabled . . . and if you become permanently disabled, your family will lose everything because you will be unable to work and they will have the added expense of taking care of you. If you carry insurance against this enormous risk, you avoid losing everything and have the ability to maintain a high standard of living no matter what happens to you."

4 | You Can't Beat Biology

If you recall, the South Africa study tested for **photos** and **similarity of last name of letter author** of lender employees who were "sending the letter," and that person's **race and gender** were manipulated depending on the race and gender of the recipient of the letter (guessed by the names of the people). Then 10,000 pieces were sent with no photo as a control for this variable.[1]

Fascinatingly, **photos of men caused people to stay home**. Far fewer people receiving letters with photos of men came in for loans.

A photo of a female employee in the letter, on the other hand, increased people coming in for a loan significantly, often by as much as the same effect as a 2.2 percent lower interest rate per month offering!

More significantly, the letter with a photo of a female employee, when sent to men, **increased the number of those coming in for a loan, so much** so that *the offer would have had to have been a 4.5 percent lower interest rate per month to generate the same result!*

More significantly yet? *When the men had previously taken out loans from the lender three or more times, the photo of a female had an even greater impact.*

Men did not positively respond to a male photo in a significant way and only slightly less so than those receiving letters with no photo at all.

---

[1] M. Bertrand, D. Karlan, S. Mullainathan, E. Shafir, and J. Zinman, "What's Psychology Worth? A Field Experiment in the Consumer Credit Market" (Yale University Economic Growth Center Discussion Paper No. 918, July 2005).

Female customers showed no significant reaction in responding to the loan offer, whether the photo was of a man, a woman, or there was no photo at all.

Many other influential variables were tested and reported on that are beyond the scope of this book. (For more information, see *What's Advertising Content Worth? Evidence From a Consumer Credit Marketing Field Experiment,* 2010.)

5 | Face Your jpeg

What if you aren't a woman, or an attractive woman? What should *you* do?

How important is your face in selling and marketing? Should you have your photo on your business card? Website? Marketing materials? Does it really make a difference?

You should absolutely put your photo on your business card, website, marketing materials, political signs, and so on. Do everything you can to ensure that people know your face, that they are familiar with it.

The brain strongly associates familiarity with attraction and positive feelings, so we want your face to be as familiar as possible. A recognized face is generally a trusted face (with a few exceptions), and you will compound the effect through repetition.

Take these actions: Put your picture on your business card. Incorporate your photo in all your advertising so that your face becomes familiar, friendly, and trustworthy—and influential as an expert in your industry.

Put a 1.5-by-1-inch photo of yourself in the upper left corner of your website. In terms of spatial dynamics, that shows the service or product is not all about you, but that you are there to help.

Insurance agents or realtors can put a black-and-white image at the top right of business stationery. With a picture of your agent present, it's harder to break a relationship with "the company."

One of the coolest ways I've seen an image used is by a neat lady named Gina, who was in my Internet Marketing class in Dallas. She had a photo of her daughter embossed on her purse. Imagine the self-esteem boost to that kid! Worth 100 "I love you's!"

6 | Compliance-Causing Questions

When you ask anyone if they intend to take some specific action, they become more likely to follow through than if they had never been asked.

And it doesn't matter if the person responds "no" or not.

Your asking and their entertaining the question creates an intention that tends to remain available to higher level "employees of you" until you have done the deed.

Now, do understand that people ask you intention questions all the time and you **do not** act on all of them. But you act on **far more** intention questions than you might think possible.

It's the way the brain is wired and how the processes all interact with each other.

If you ask someone, "Will you buy a Mac before Christmas?" that someone is much more likely to buy a Mac than the person you asked, "Will you buy a computer before Christmas?" The second person is much more likely to buy a computer than the person you asked nothing of.

A one-second question will very probably cause them to buy a new laptop, or in the first case a Mac, much more often than you or they would have predicted.

The employees of you are fast at work. And they do keep track of information.

As soon as you buy the computer, the employee pulls the constant nagging reminders about computer purchases and the notion is forgotten.

Let's get more precise here.

"Are you going to go to dinner with me this month?"

You ask that question and the other person now has an employee (a part) in charge of making certain that she goes out to dinner with you.

She may not. It may not be possible. She might be repulsed! But the nagging employee doesn't pay attention to such things.

The employee's job is to make sure that outcome of going to dinner this month is fulfilled. Once the month is over or the person has indeed gone out to dinner, the nagging has ceased and the person has peace of mind again.

Have you ever heard the saying "The squeaky wheel gets the grease"?

Human behavior is often codified with some accuracy in sayings or stories of folklore.

As you can see asking one question of someone can be a causal element for life-changing behavior.

And you also now understand that where you don't paint a complete picture, the other person's brain has an employee to do just that.

If you know what is likely to be drawn based on your knowledge of the individual, their behavior, their personal history, their attitudes, and beliefs, the simplest of ambiguous questions can generate the most profound behaviors.

Carefully crafted questions can have significant persuasive impact.

7 | Direct the Traffic

When a well-formed leading question is asked, it is usually answered without further argument. When it is answered, it **leads** the person one small step forward in the thought-direction you are taking them.

Having just experienced jury duty, I'm compelled to use this example.

Attorneys ask leading questions to establish momentum and at the same time *avoid* any of the information that does not flatter their case.

"Were you at the house at 8:40 p.m.?"

"Yes."

"Did you have a loud argument?"

"Yes."

These are very good questions to establish facts as you see them and build momentum as you build the path to the actions you want the other to take.

Too many leading questions can begin to feel like an interrogation.

The most effective way to use these to help the other person decide is to map out a set of questions and possible answers that help you cause the person to realize what they need to do next.

Leading questions have been shown to actually change a "memory" of what a person believes he witnessed.

According to E. Loftus and J. Palmer, the questions asked after an event, seemingly designed to *help* a witness recall what they remember seeing or experiencing, can actually be structured to introduce new information or doubt in what is asserted by the witness.

This is certainly easy to see in a courtroom. Here, the prosecution can only ask questions of the witness. And it is here that very subtle differences in wording can produce shockingly different results.

Let's turn back to Loftus for a moment. In one of her experiments, after subjects were shown a video of a car accident, they were asked one of five questions:

1. How fast were the cars going when they smashed into each other?
2. How fast were the cars going when they collided into each other?
3. How fast were the cars going when they bumped into each other?
4. How fast were the cars going when they hit each other?
5. How fast were the cars going when they contacted each other?

With the above question, "smashed" produced the highest estimated speed. The scale slides down to "contacted," which was the lowest estimated speed.

So, realize there are different degrees of impact in each word that is used within each question. Words can matter. Some word choices are simply stronger at conveying meaning. Choose carefully as you are quite literally *leading* the thoughts of the others in your world.

8 | Do I Understand?

When necessary, discover precisely what their words mean to them.

One trap we commonly fall into is thinking that everyone has the same definition of the words we all use every day. They do not.

When we experience anything, we label it with words. Think about the last time something happened that you wanted to tell your best friend. In that moment, you are wrapping words around the experience and, in effect, "labeling" it. Those labels are the words that mean something to you. How you define what those words mean is unique to you and might be completely different from another person who also experienced the same event and is telling one of *his* friends.

Differences in definition cause misunderstandings. In your communication, it is critical then to ask the right questions to either help define the situation in the manner that is helpful to you, or at the very least question to understand how the other person is defining the event.

What triggers you to ask defining questions is the feeling you get after you paraphrase and feedback what you believe they are telling you. Their reaction will give you a clue if you are on the same page.

If you don't clarify—right now, in this moment—then that person will leave the encounter with you and say, do, or believe things that are not in line with the direction you would like to have them moving.

For example: If the person describes the situation as "overwhelming," ask, "What exactly do you mean by 'overwhelming'?" With the focus placed on this word, you are forcing a description of what "overwhelming" means to them. The more you understand this, the better chance you have to successfully persuade them.

Listen for the words they use to describe the situation:

Exciting
Frustrating
Confusing
Disappointing

Also listen for the words they use to describe how they *feel* about the situation:

Tired
Frustrated
Overwhelmed
Overloaded
Fried
Baked
Burnt out
Encouraged
Optimistic

With these two key pieces of information: (1) how they describe what the situation means to them and (2) how they describe how they *feel* about that situation, you begin to "'speak their language'," lower defenses, and lead them to the best solution.

Here's an example:

Customer: "I just can't afford this plan. It's too expensive."
You: "Expensive in what way?"

The chances are that they will either define expensive as:

- An unnecessary luxury or one that is not seen as fitting with their image or status.
- Overpriced, compared to perceived value.
- Out of their current budget.

Once you have that information, you can work to modify their perception of the benefits or select a more suitable alternative choice.

Definition questions are also used to clarify items that could be an objection for you or the other person.

When you need to clarify, ask:

"Can you tell me more about why it's necessary to involve Bob?"

This will get the person to clarify Bob's role and why it is important to have him on the project. The person may have been on the fence about Bob, but after clarifying his value, it cements Bob's position on the project team.

Another goal in clarifying definitions is to use their answer as a positive lead into a clarifying statement by you. For example:

You: [if the other person didn't mention quality and you know this is critical] "Of all those factors you just mentioned, what about the speed is important?"

Jenn: "Speed is critical; it's the only factor that matters because it keeps the per-piece price down."

You: "So the per-piece price is more important than the quality of each piece?"

Jenn: "Oh, no, the quality of each piece is the most important because it doesn't matter how inexpensive each piece is if they are no good.

You: "Got it. I understand your point. Quality is the priority."

Clarifications of definition allow you to gently steer the focus of the other person in the direction that will keep their thoughts and actions in line with the outcomes the other person needs.

9

The First Shall Be Last and the Last Shall Be First

Sequencing matters, as you learned earlier. But there is more to consider than just the sequence itself.

When presenting an idea, lead with a statement of the benefit and the results that can be expected from what you propose, then progress, using discovery questions so that the other person is answering questions and telling you stories about why they want what you are offering.

In the majority of circumstances, the option(s) noted last is not only remembered first, but chosen or decided in the end. The next most common choice is what is offered first.

It turns out that when people are in a good mood, they tend to accept what is offered to them first.

When people aren't in a good mood, they tend to ruminate and all things being equal they are more likely to select what is last.

If you have the option of being one presenter of many today, you'll want to go first or last and use the above criteria for deciding when you want to speak.

When is typically far more important than **what** or **how**.

10 | More Than the Message

When planning the delivery of your message, remember that the outcome of the delivery is dependent on a lot more than just the message.

There is also context, environment, and peripheral puzzle pieces that aren't the core of the messenger's information.

Nonprofit organizations will often send out attractive women to do their fundraising or recruiting in order to increase the number of people who become involved and amount of dollars donated. When the woman makes her presentation to a group, the content of her message receives some attention, which will be influential on the final decision-making. But for many people in the audience, the fact that she is attractive will add dramatic weight to the decision for many if not all in the group.

Select the right environment.

Influence is not only about the messenger. It's about where and how the message is being delivered.

Are you in a church, a school, at a playground, at a bar, a nightclub, or in an office building? The same message in all of those places will be received differently and will lead to different decisions due to the influence of the location. Pick your location carefully.

Who is the messenger with?

When the man is walking down the hall or accompanied on a business meeting by an attractive lady, she is peripheral to him but adds great value to him.

Your car.

The car you arrive in has an enormous impact if they see you stepping out of the car and it does not meet with their approval.

Some examples:

If it's a gas-guzzling vehicle, you lose if you are talking to an environmentalist.

Perhaps you arrived in a minivan, and you will be meeting with a wealthy single executive.

Perhaps you arrive in a Jaguar, and you will be speaking to a conservative religious family.

In all cases, the car works against the messenger.

Always think about more than just you and the other person. Everything else matters. Be certain everything is as you plan.

11

When All Else Fails

Not all questions designed to cause change or motivate are phrased gently or delicately.

Dramatically blunt communication bypasses all arguments, objections, options, choices, or emotional processing and causes the other person to make a dramatic choice.

Examples:

"Kevin, I can't afford life insurance."

"Okay, so am I getting this straight? So you die and there's your wife and kids and a year ago you said, 'Gee I can't afford $300!' and they could have had $250,000 but you left them broke?"

"Kevin, I can't afford fresh fruit and vegetables."

"So it's okay to sacrifice the health of your kids for whatever else you spent money on in the house? So there's something more important than the health of your kids? That's what I'm supposed to understand, right?"

The whole point of this type of conversation is that it is contentious. It breaks through and gets straight to the most valued dimension of the matter: helping the person clearly visualize where their focus should be placed.

The aim is highly compassionate. The aim is to have you experience what you need to with complete clarity so that you avoid a painful future and the deeper pain of regret.

12

Something Money Can't Buy

It is natural for everyone to respond negatively to an opportunity. We do it naturally, without a great deal of thought and conscious cognition. That is Reactance. Reactance is the visceral reaction that avoids being manipulated. It avoids having choices removed, even though most people make better decisions with fewer choices. It's just another one of the ironies of the influence experience.

A large percentage of negotiations come down to something related to money.

But the fact is there is a lot more than money in a negotiation.

My friend Ronald from Brussels worked in the training department for a major European private bank. The bank had hired me the previous year to do a two-day training in Amsterdam. It went splendidly.

Their training budget for this year was not all about Kevin Hogan. They actually had the audacity to have other expenses such as an expensive hotel, feeding 140 high-net-worth individuals' account executives for three days, and other required expenditures.

Ronald had balked at the price the year before. Of course, he's supposed to do that.

This year I asked for a bit more than last, but Ronald actually had to come under budget.

"Kevin, you are a man of the world" (whatever that meant). "There is more to life than money. How much would it be worth for you to meet the VP of Sales and Marketing at Maserati in Italy?"

Everyone knows I'm not a car guy. I didn't even know what a Maserati looked like. I had no idea what European girls see when they see a Maserati.

Answering this question was simple:

"You can't put a price on something like that, Ronald."

I thought he was going to ask me if it was worth $5,000 for a minute. Seeing he hadn't hit my hottest of hot buttons, he put this on the table:

"Kevin, Mr. Roenke wants to make sure you personally get a tour of the Maserati plant and watch a car being made by hand. Only VIPs and people who spend 200,000 to 500,000 euros on their car get this treatment. Now how would (x dollars) plus that experience you'll never get again in your lifetime be for you?"

"I'll see you in April, Ronald. Send over the paperwork."

I was on my way to Italy for the price of an event in the United States. Ronald Vertseegen was a pretty sharp guy. He reframed the entire situation by providing *huge* benefit up front *before* the bad news of the reduced speaking fee.

13 | Attention → Here

A good, sharp "filter question" will direct the other person's thoughts in a very precisely predetermined direction.

The following are examples of **filter questions**:

"How would things have been different if you had never met (person A)?"
"What is good about the way things have turned out?"
"How did your parents prepare you for situations like this?"
"Who would be the best person to help you in this situation?"
"What would be the outcome if you believed X instead?"
"What would be different if X were not true?"
"Could there be another right answer here?"
"If there were another solution here, what could it be?"

You use filter questions to place attention on a specific place, time, solution, or other feature. You are creating the assumption that the answer to the question mirrors the way you have framed it.

14 | Imagined Ownership

People value what they have and want more of it. Then when they want to sell it, they want a lot more than they paid for it. *It had gone up in value.*

It's no secret that people place big prices on things they are going to sell. Similarly we all tend to value ourselves more than others value us.

In a retail store it's pretty easy to get someone to pick up something, feel attachment, and have them walk out of the store a happy owner of the product.

It's more difficult in other settings.

Direct marketers "guarantee" results and use tactics such as "90 days same-as-cash" and risk-free guarantees that are all designed to allow ownership, to allow us the chance to experience the value and realize that it is beyond the cost of the money to get it.

How can you induce imagined ownership?

Create a frame (a word picture in their mind) that you (or your product, service, or idea) are something that they already possess so that it becomes the status quo in their thinking.

"Once our lawn service is yours, we help you eliminate all that crabgrass, the crabgrass all your old services said they would get rid of but couldn't even keep under control!"

In order to implement this technique the other person *must* sense or perceive ownership of a decision, item, idea, or service.

You can also spend a little time with someone descr__
what it would be like *for them* to have, use, own, and be
product or service, and very briefly what it would be like for
ally if they didn't have, do, or believe the way you want them
sound something like this:

"What do you think the biggest benefit could be for you?"

This question conveys to them that they need to tell you
value most. It could be anything, and from this point forward in
munication, your goal is to spend a couple of seconds in the future
person enjoying how nice it would be to have that benefit. Then ri__
that inject a sharp contrast by pulling that same benefit away. Make
that without a decision today, they will never have that enjoyable futt

This makes it easy for them to say "yes" to you as you have lit__
shifted the value-scale to the point where the amount of money nece__
seems smaller to enjoy a benefit that now *seems* larger than it did ju__
minute ago.

15

Unique Frame Precludes "No"

Your best framing is often accomplished with well-formed questions. Think carefully about what you want that answer to be and what direction you want that answer to lead. Then ask the set-up question that frames the next exchange:

"Kevin, your candidate actually has a chance of winning this time. If we could just get some more support, we could take a probable 49 percent and tip it to a 51 percent or better. I know you don't want the opposition party to win, with all the extra red tape, expenses, and problems that it's going to cause you and your business. I more than understand that you're a busy guy, but can I count on your help to make some calls over a couple of days and get this pushed through? Can I count on you to make some phone calls for us this week to encourage people to vote? They may not listen to anyone but you."

The example above is clearly constructed to get Kevin to say yes to making phone calls to likely voters on behalf of the campaign. It's much more effective than simply saying, "Kev, can you make some phone calls to help get Johnston elected?"

Using the word "win" was central to getting Kevin to help with the phone calls. There's a dramatic difference in the language we use to influence. Words really matter.

A difference in the description of hamburger as either "75 percent lean" or "25 percent fat" dramatically changes the sales of each, and it's **exactly the same product**.

Not only does the phrase sound different, but it also produces significantly different outcomes. Can you guess which one sells more beef? You're right if you said "75 percent lean."

People don't want to buy fat: they want to buy lean. That's a simple but strong frame to remember going forward.

16

The Contrastive Analysis

One of my favorite influential triggers to agreement is eliciting contrast from another person.

Contrast is consistently predictable in generating compliance. It is most effective in situations where rational thinking and logic will prevail. It can be adapted to situations where emotions will make the difference, as you can see in the example below.

Bring mental images in their mind close together by showing Option A, then Option B, and quickly moving on.

If you can remember your last visit to the optometrist, you did this in discovering the correction needed for your eyes.

Imagine a guy talking to his potential date:

Kevin: "So how come you're sitting here with me instead of with some really good-looking man? What happened to the last guy you were with?"

Kim: "Ohhh . . . he turned out to be a real jerk."

Kevin: "Like how?"

Kim: "He was rude, said inappropriate things in front of my girlfriends, and flirted with them."

Kevin: "And how about the guy before that?"

Kim: "He was a jerk, too. Always waking me up by texting me in the
          middle of the night. Really controlling. He even showed up at my
          office when I didn't call him back one day."
Kevin: "A lot of guys can be really insensitive like that—it seems pretty
          normal from what I hear. What about the one before that?"
Kim: "You mean the one who hit on my sister?"
Kevin: "So what are you going to do to stop this insanity?"
Kim: "I'm being a lot more picky about who I date now. They have to
          pass a bunch of personality tests first."
Kevin: "Well, in that case I'll stick around. . . . "

Practice this kind of contrastive analysis often so when you meet that
girl you are able to communicate elegantly, revealing a sense of certainty
and personal magnetism rarely seen in others.

17 | Give Them a Cup of Coffee

Today they are going to make a hundred decisions, or so it will appear to most people around them. Of the 100 decisions they will make, perhaps five were actually "considered." For the other 95 decisions, they instinctively reacted to a given set of circumstances and said yes or no based upon how they *felt*.

When someone has said yes based on "instinct," it's often difficult for them to then logically justify what they just did and stick with it. This is why there are so many people who say, "I changed my mind . . . I decided not to . . . I checked the budget and I can't afford it . . . My old boyfriend asked me out and I decided to go with him."

One part wanted X. One part wanted anything *but* X.

The error that the influencer often makes when the other person agrees quickly is that they have made an emotional decision and that this specific yes is in concrete. Not the case. One part of the person, forward in the moment, compelled the individual to rapid agreement. That was an ancient, brain-based **reaction**. It was representative of a part of that person. Now you need to get them to justify and rationalize why they just said yes.

If you can do that, the other person will have no resistance to you. They have no reactance to your communication. This decision is all but set in stone.

In the other 95 percent of decisions that the person makes, they are leaning toward no based upon how they feel around you. They are uncomfortable; they don't want to be taken advantage of. They don't want to look stupid in front of the neighbors. They don't want the girl next door thinking you ended up with the wrong partner.

So if a decision is going to be made based on rational consideration, the person has to rationalize what their emotions are telling them.

As long as the other person is still talking to you about your proposal, this means they are still oscillating between yes and no. The single most common reason people say no is that they don't want to be taken advantage of. In consumer scenarios, this means they don't want to have spent too much money on something. In almost all cases when people are *asked* to buy something, the decision comes down to "Do I really need it?" or "It's going to cost me too much money." The ironic piece of life's puzzle here is that, had the person simply bought instead of being *asked* to buy, they would have bought solely on impulse.

Dealing with money or price isn't as difficult as it's made out to be. People hear a big number like $1,000 and they get nervous. But research shows that people will have their decision directed to yes if the dollar figure is reduced to a ridiculously small amount of money per day. A few bonus percentage points can be added by further framing the choice in contrast to something they use many times in the course of a day, that having one fewer wouldn't cause a sense of loss.

For example, a cup of coffee costs around $3. Your $1,000 is really $3 a day for the rest of the year. So now the person can feel quite good that they are going from five cups of coffee per day to four cups a day—something they should be doing anyway, and using that $3 per day to purchase your item.

It's very important to not take away something they only have one of every day. If they only have one doughnut per day, you do not want to take that away. Assuming the individual is a coffee drinker, they probably drink three to four cups a day and now they can painlessly buy the widget they've wanted.

A couple of examples:

"This new program costs $1,000. By utilizing it, you should increase your small business sales by $25,000 to $30,000 over a period of five years. So for the price of your daily cup of coffee, you could be getting yourself something really huge."

"The subscription costs $99 a year. Essentially for a few pennies per day, you'll have complete access to the Money Report, showing you how to achieve a 7 to 10 percent return on your investments. What's that? $50,000 per year?"

18 | The $4,000,000 Bra

Each year Victoria's Secret puts their most beautiful model wearing a $4 million bejeweled bra on the cover of their catalog. The dramatic image makes it impossible to not pick up the catalog and get another look inside.

That $4 million bra creates a dramatic distinction between what could possibly be spent today instead of the $75 they will actually spend.

In numerous research studies in catalog promotions, the addition of an extremely expensive high-end product causes people to buy the next highest inexpensive product with a great degree of consistency.

You can use the same method to make the price of a relationship with the other person too expensive, making a relationship with you the more likely choice. This is accomplished by eliciting what people don't want in a relationship and finding which of those things your competitor has.

Perhaps they have young children and you do not.

Perhaps they have no real future prospects and you do.

Perhaps they have an ex-wife with a history of reckless behavior and you don't.

Those are all potentially big prices to pay to be in a relationship.

19 | Mirror Neuron on the Wall . . .

It appears that mirror neurons are at the heart of empathy. Empathy is certainly at the heart of influence. When you look at other people, listen to other people, feel other people, mirror neurons activate and translate what that person is experiencing to you.

Empathy is invisible. To be empathetic with the other person's situation endears you to them, breaks down resistance, and helps them feel that you are more like them, and therefore the suggestions you make are more influential.

Empathy is arguably the single most important factor in influencing others.

Empathy is the ability to feel . . . to understand . . . to walk a mile in their shoes. Empathy means that you can feel and see life from the perspective of the other person. If and when you can do that, you can be influential. You can build a strong rapport that can act as the basis of your recommendation and carry significant weight.

You could employ all the techniques in this book, but if you can't feel what they feel, you will never truly be a person of great influence.

Imagine you're watching the CNN coverage of the torrential rains and severe flooding in Myanmar back in 2008: You see a woman with her two young children as the floods sweep in. She is separated at an almost equal distance from each one of them. Each is being taken away in an opposite direction. She has to act fast but . . . she can save only one of her children. That was one of the toughest things I've ever watched. That kind of empathy is hard on the soul.

People with high levels of empathy have three common traits:

1. They have experienced pain firsthand.
2. They have a wide range of experiences with all kinds of other people.
3. They are validated and feel good based upon the approval of the others.

The way to connect to the other person is by being empathic. The way is to always be supportive, kind, and helpful, and draw on the emotions within you that are the same as those being experienced by the other person.

Ask yourself, "What is this person feeling right now?" Expand your awareness beyond just the matter at hand. Become aware of everything else they've let you know is going on in their life on numerous levels. None of us make it through a year without significant changes and life events, so the chances are you will only occasionally be meeting with a person who is truly happy and problem-free. At best they may be having a neutral moment. Expect that everyone has challenges and is hurting to some degree. Once you start from that point of view, you can then judge what opinions and feelings you think they are having about this particular decision.

We all want to be understood and liked by others. People who are empathetic make it a point to understand others and look out for the interests of everyone.

In personal interactions, it's true that people don't buy the product or service; they buy *you*. And just what is that "you"? It's your understanding of them that they see from how you mirrored them.

The person of influence is the one with great empathy for the other. They are inherently kind. They certainly can be disciplined in approach. They can be tough as nails or soft as kittens.

Want to check your level of empathy? Grab a friend and a video camera, and record them telling you something that's troubling them. Then start talking and record your response. Watch it through to the end and make a note of your verbal and nonverbal responses, and ask your friend for feedback.

20 | Behavioral Gravity

People's behavior often tends to be inconsistent with what it was just minutes ago. For example, if someone just had an expensive, but healthy, salad for lunch, no dressing, and a glass of water, and they then pass a gift shop on the way back to the office, they are more likely to indulge in buying a gift for themselves or somebody else.

The reason was that they exercised restraint and that they will now make up for it.

So, if your goal is to get your spouse to quit spending so much and blowing the household budget, take them out for a big steak dinner with plenty of wine, a tasty crème brûlée for dessert, and then say, "Hey, I've got a question for you. I realized when I looked at the credit card statement this month, that I spent $197 being subscribed to the WSJ this year. I had no idea it was that expensive, and I felt bad so I cancelled. What else would you like me to cut back on for us to save money each month?"

You then accept a very long list about your overspending. Because the person who indulged first their natural human bias is now to be careful and conservative, they will come up with suggestions for their own cutbacks.

You combine that with the fact that you have asked them to help you cut your budget. You offer *no* suggestions, but simply ask questions such as "You really think that's possible?"

Before you know it, they have talked themselves into an overhaul of spending that includes their own areas of responsibility. Don't tell anyone I told you this one. . . .

21 | If You Insist

You know you have done your job when you're trying to persuade someone to X and they start talking as if X were their own idea.

How exactly do you bring the person there?

A simple question.

Questions have a compelling nature that begs them to be answered and what you ask determines the type of answers you will get.

The answer is their way of drawing conclusions. When they generate the answer, they are in control, and they will be more personally committed to the outcome. They will monitor their own actions resulting from it, because it was *their idea*.

So when you present your ideas, deliberately leave a concluding piece of information out, but lay the groundwork of all the facts around it, so the outcome you want is the only conclusion they can come to.

It might sound like this:

Kevin: "I was thinking about asking you to go and see *Dark Knight Rises,* but you've probably seen that, so I thought maybe *Finding Nemo* in 3D, but then I said, 'She probably doesn't want to see a kids' movie.' So I thought about the one with that guy who plays Thor in the Avenger, what's it called? Something about a fairytale?"

Katie: "*Snow White and the Huntsman.*"
Kevin: "Yeah that's the one, *Snow White and the Huntsman.* Let's go to that one."

This does several things. First, it does not say that you are asking her out on a date. Secondly, resistance is lowered by getting her to name the movie, almost as if she were suggesting it. All you are then doing is accepting their suggestion.

22

Here's the Message for That Mood

Knowing as much as you can about the other person *before* you make any communication is critical. You can dramatically increase your success by noticing, in this case, the mood of the other person.

Research has found that if that other person is in a down or sad mood, your message will be received as more persuasive than it otherwise might be, depending on how you position it.

It's all about cognitive load, or how much information people are processing.

Happy or angry people, in other words, those who are in an activated or impulsive mood, make decisions faster, so you can lay out your preferred choices as early on as possible.

In contrast, the person who is sad, hurt, fearful, depressed, or otherwise negative is handling information slower in one of these emotional states. So you need to present them with your preferred choice later in the proposal.

It might sound like this when talking to someone who seems downcast:

The Roofer: "Kevin, you have two choices. The storm has taken off about a third of the shingles on the roof. If we just replace those shingles, we're looking at about $10,000 out of pocket, as your insurance deductible is just greater than $10,000.

"The other option would be to get your insurance to pay for most of a new roof, because when their adjuster gets out here they're going to declare it a total loss, and the cost to you is still going to be $10,000. Your house—what do you want me to do?"

23 | Behavioral Integration

If you can get the other person to physically make the movements that lead to the desired emotion or action, they will soon feel it or do it of their own accord.

Research shows that the artificial creation of smiling made study participants rate cartoons as funnier than those whose faces were not forced into a smile.

Here's how you can utilize this:

"If you don't mind, Madison, I'd like to unroll this poster right here on your desk. Can you come around and take a look at it with me? It outlines every step of the process we have been talking about."

Or:

"Could you please hold this sample, Mackenzie? I've got to get the other one out of the box."

In both examples above, you're causing the other person to physically move. You are changing their perspective by physically integrating them. By doing this, you have an excellent opportunity to engage them on a deeper level. With more engagement comes much easier influence.

When I do a presentation I all but demand that participants take handwritten notes. Taking notes involves many influential processes. One is that it encourages learning. A second is that it engenders better memory. And if they are writing something down it, and therefore, you *must be important*.

24

Have Them Help You Help Them Change

Almost every company in the Dow (stock market) from, say 75 years ago, is long gone. Security is built on **change** and not the status quo, but **your client believes that the status quo is the only security there is.**

This obviously does not open the door to new ideas or actions, so you need to help them move away from the status quo.

Here are four messages your client should be caused to communicate to you in your meeting:

1. Disadvantages and Pessimism of the Status Quo
2. Advantages of Change
3. Optimism for Change
4. Intention to Change

Your client can communicate all four of the above elements to you in a fashion that makes it obvious that *staying the course will ultimately lead to disaster.*

They must tell you what is wrong with the status quo *in their own words, not yours.* They must tell you the advantages of change. They must share with you optimism for change, even if it is simply acknowledging that it is better than what they have right now. Finally they must intend to change internally.

(Then, of course, they must change.)

Whether your client goes to the medical doctor, the life insurance gal, or the real estate guy, these things must all happen for change to have *any* chance of sticking.

When you ask questions, you don't have every answer or solution ready to bash them over the head, but you have the ability to figure out the solution with your client.

Are you familiar with the story I sometimes tell of the wife who tries for hours to fix a light at home?

The guy comes home from work. She's in a bad mood. He's fine. She tells him how hard her day has been trying to fix this thing. He walks over to it and immediately turns a screw and, poof! It works instantly. That should make the world a better place and the wife happy, right?

You've got to be kidding.

People need to *feel competent*. They don't only want a result. Absolutely, positively *not*.

People do not only want results . . . they want feelings and experiences as well.

They don't only want a problem solved. They want to feel competent and as if they are part of the solution. If you fail to accomplish this, you will lose far more often than you win even though you immediately solve their problem.

The prospective client doesn't want to be boxed in to your box with you. They must **have** and **feel** freedom to think, feel intelligent, experience self-esteem when talking to you, and **know** that you get their business, life, problems before they say yes to you.

Here's what I do when I am communicating with a prospective client about speaking with their group at a meeting or perhaps giving a training in influence or body language.

I formulate a series of questions. Some of these are relevant to my fee, but most aren't. Most are relevant to the content of my presentation and what the current state of the company, department, or association is. I'm always sensitive to the reality that the person I'm talking to doesn't want to share a lot of this information that is private. I also know (and so do they) that if they don't tell me this information they will get just another motivational speech that takes 100 people away from their job for a couple of hours and gets them nothing in return for a couple of hours.

- What is the purpose of the meeting?
- What are you hoping to accomplish?
- Who else will be speaking? About what?
- Why did you contact me instead of someone else?
- What do you want me to communicate to your audience?
- What is the greatest benefit to you of bringing me into your company?
- If we were successful in increasing cohesion, compliance, and improving skills, would you be interested in a mutually beneficial long-term relationship?

Those questions show the planner that she has contacted the right person. Create your own discovery process that leads to you so you can have them help you help them change.

25 | The Second Right Answer

Sometimes we try to get to the second right answer because the first reaction is usually not the best possible answer.

It is certainly true that your gut instinct can produce some very good instant assessments of familiar situations. But the problem is that most people will stop right there, usually without giving it a thought. They simply stop thinking. They get an idea or an answer, and they just go with it.

There is an opportunity for you to bring the person to a better answer by asking a careful question to generate more thought. Quite simply it helps them realize that there are other options and that there just may be a better way

It may sound like this:

"Marc, that's good, especially in light of the fact the budget just got cut." (I can see how you came to your decision.) "What other options do we have?" (I want you to come up with more ideas just in case there is an even better solution than that.)

This type of question validates their first answer, but then asks them to find more options in a specific area. Once they do this, they will come up with answers very close to what would be in their best interest, and they will feel it will be their idea.

Similar questions to generate other options include:

"What else is true?"
"If that is so, wouldn't ____ also be true?"
"What other use could this have?"
"How can we use this to make ____ happen?"

26 | Hypothetically Speaking

The skillful use of a hypothetical situation can help the other person to see past obstacles or roadblocks in a way that otherwise wouldn't be possible and can also help the other person to see things your way without any reactance.

Hypothetical questions are really asking, "What if?"

They fit smoothly into conversations and are such strong thought-directors that they are one of the more valuable forms of influence. Here are some examples:

"Would it be possible to _____?"
"How would you do it if _____?"
"If X were true, what would you do?"
"What if _____?"

Questions like this typically refer to a *potential future* based on some current assumptions.

Remember, this is only a potential future. With the right guidance, there can be a better outcome, and the future that unfolds can be better than the other person imagined.

This is one of the approaches that nonprofit fundraising will use from time to time showing what *will* happen with your donations and what will happen *without* your donations. They paint a hypothetical picture with emotion that often results in a steady stream of donations.

27 | Switching Labels

Everyone is snobby about something. Some people only wear Nike, drink Red Bull, or won't own anything but an iPhone.

You can wear the same clothes for years, but when some other group of people starts to wear the clothes that your group wears, you switch to another brand!

You and I behave in certain ways because those behaviors define our identity. As soon as the products we use fail to differentiate us from others we do not want to be identified with, we change our choices.

If you want someone to switch brands or guys, make sure they see the brand they are using being used by people they don't respect and don't admire. The word picture should be so glaring that it causes them to feel a sense of embarrassment. They aren't part of that group and never want to be associated with it.

More Thinking without Thinking

Changing the label on a wine changed diners' opinions of their wine, opinions of their meal, and their repatronage of the restaurant, according to a Cornell University study.

Forty-one diners at the Spice Box restaurant in Urbana, Illinois, were given a free glass of Cabernet Sauvignon to accompany a $24 prix-fixe French meal. Half the bottles claimed to be from Noah's Winery in California. The labels on the other half claimed to be from Noah's Winery in North Dakota. In both cases, the wine was an inexpensive Charles Shaw wine.

Those drinking what they thought was California wine rated the wine and food as tasting better, and ate 11 percent more of their food. They were also more likely to make return reservations.

It comes down to expectations. If you think a wine is a good wine, whether "good wine" means what the other person dining with you thinks about you for ordering it or not, it will taste better than if you think it will taste bad.

People didn't believe North Dakota wine would taste good, so it had a double curse—it hurt both the wine and the entire meal. "Wine labels can throw both a halo or a shadow over the entire dining experience," according to Cornell Professor Brian Wansink (PhD), author of *Mindless Eating: Why We Eat More Than We Think* (Bantam, 2006).

To confirm this, a similar study was conducted with 49 MBA students at a wine and cheese reception. Again, those given wine labeled from California rated the wine as 85 percent higher and the cheese as 50 percent higher.

It's not the wine that tastes good or bad. It's the perception. It's the reputation North Dakota has with the average wine drinker. That perception is not good. The average wine drinker doesn't want to be associated with North Dakota. The North Dakota wine could be the best tasting wine in history, but the reputation and perception of North Dakota reveals the power of labels.

Labels Are Frames

Use word pictures to reframe. Here's what she is thinking:

"Oh my God, he just told the waiter he wanted a bottle of North Dakota wine. If anyone saw that I'll never be able to come back here again . . . and even if they didn't, I'll never go out with this guy again."

28

Listen for What They're Not Saying

Sometimes you'll be face to face with that important person and you'll become aware that what you wanted to influence them about is not the most important thing in their life today. Perhaps you are asking the girl for a date and she is seemingly on the fence. She can't quite say yes or no. You get a strange sense.

You ask, "You've got something on your mind. What's up?"

It's here that you might get a response like this:

"My mom is in the hospital. She's been real sick and I'm worried about her. I just don't know how she'll be doing by Friday."

"You need someone to come by and take Sparky out so you can spend the day with your mom? We can go out any day. You need to get your mom well."

The question you asked had nothing to do with your desire for a date and whether it would be accepted. If you have lost out at this point for some reason, so be it, but you've been valuable to your friend and that is likely to be viewed favorably.

Obviously these same kinds of experiences happen in business, in negotiations, and relationships of all kinds.

What they are not saying can make all the difference in the world.

29 | Role-Response-Projection

If you want someone to behave in a fashion that's different from how they have in the past, or if you want someone to do something specific, use Role-Response-Projection.

This works by assigning traits or characteristics to a person or group that they will then feel compelled to adopt or compelled to avoid. This is effective when the person sees themselves benefiting in some way. The benefit could be tangible (such as receiving money) or intangible (such as gaining respect or love).

For example, a man is pursuing a woman for a date and has engaged her in a short conversation. Because she isn't absolutely sure of this one, she doesn't want to be pressured so she says, "You know what I like about you? You like to listen. You seem sensitive and not high pressure like so many other guys. I appreciate that."

Instantly the gears start shifting inside the mind of that man. This isn't where he was going, but if he wants this woman, it's the *role she is projecting for him* that she finds acceptable, if not preferable.

He may reply, "Men can be such jerks. I've never understood how men can be so insecure that they have to demand something of a woman that she isn't even ready to give."

With Role-Response-Projection, she projects the role onto him that she wants him to fit into. The interesting thing is that not only is this tactic effective, it can be the easiest and most invisible way to change behavior in the long term with just a small amount of repetition and reinforcement.

You explicitly say what you want in a completely nonthreatening way. It causes the person to understand and accept the role you want them to play.

The Reciprocal Response Projection

There is a flip-side of this technique that sounds like this: "I'd **never** go out with a guy who . . ." Whatever she says next will immediately alter and direct the behavior of the man who wants to be perceived by her as desirable.

If he wants to date her, he'll comply with the projection.

30 | Let Them Direct the Traffic

Sometimes you need to influence someone in the presence of their regular source of influence, when that person may have been a contributor to their current failure. Here's a neat way of taking care of the feelings and needs of both to be validated.

We're at the pediatrician's office. The doctor says:

"Okay, the chart shows Annie is currently 110 pounds, which at 10 years old, 4 feet and 4 inches gives us a BMI of 28.6. The concern here is that she's prediabetic. We ran a test for blood sugar level and that came back at just over 100. It's not terrible, but we want to tackle this before it gets more serious. So, what do you guys want to do as far as reducing those blood sugar levels?"

He grabs a pen and paper and writes down everything the parents say, repeating their answers as he takes notes.

"Stop her having snack after school, uh-huh, stop her having bedtime snack . . . Good. Keep going . . . Let's get about 15 possible ideas and then we'll pick the top three or four that are most likely to work quickly. . . . "

After he takes all the parents' suggestions he summarizes:

"Okay, we want her to be happy and feel rewarded when she gets home, so we're not going to stop that snack after school, and the bedtime snack is probably still a good idea because when you're a kid it's pretty tough to be hungry and try and fall asleep. But look at this one, remove morning juice; right there that's 14 grams of sugar. In fact, if you remove all juice and replace that with water, that would probably solve the problem.

"We also want you to slow down dinner for the whole family, stay at the table for about 30 minutes together, and put down your knives and forks between bites and really chew that food. That helps to signal the stomach that it is full, instead of getting too much food into the body in five minutes. Annie, who are your heroes? Which posters do you have up on the wall? Justin Bieber? Katy Perry? How do you think they stay fit and healthy? They dance and work out, eat smart, not too much candy, maybe one soda a day, fruits and vegetables. Good answers, Annie! You're a smart girl, so every time you look at their posters, I want you to remember that."

Another way you can use this is in a group setting, where it appears you have read their minds in order to come up with a perfect solution. It's a great persuasion technique used by mind readers and psychics around the world.

You've been brought into a company as a consultant to help tackle a troubling rise in customer complaints. There are 12 people in the room, only a small number of whom have actually been receiving the poor customer ratings. The Customer Service manager who hired you is also present.

"We know that customer satisfaction is a complex thing, and your company is different; you guys have some unique interactions with your customers that don't fit all the rules. So I need your help. You're the ones sitting there on the phone all day. I'm an expert, but not in your job, so tell me, what is the number one thing that most of the people in this room can do to help the customers and reduce the level of complaints? What is the number one thing that you can say to a customer on the phone that will put them at ease and trust you so that they don't generate a complaint to the Better Business Bureau? What is the best question that you can ask your customer to find out what's really driving him or her nuts, so you can get them to vent and then provide them with relief? I need you to write down whatever comes to mind on those sheets I've passed out."

The consultant collects all the information, sits down, and starts looking through the feedback. He looks at each sheet, nods, and starts writing on his own pad. He does this for each person's contribution, occasionally asking people for clarification or to read something he can't decipher.

The consultant then appears to summarize the input of the most common or popular answers provided at the meeting, but what he is actually reading has been agreed between him and the Customer Service Manager, plus one or two good ideas that were generated.

"So, here's what we're going to do: [items 1, 2, 3, 4, 5, 6, 7]. Anyone want to add anything else? What you guys decided to do here is what you want, is that right? Now can you all walk me through what this would actually sound like when you are on the phone with a customer?"

The consultant gets each person to verbalize one of the things in order to own a piece of the plan. You now have an audience-generated prescription.

31 | Absorb Them into Your World

You need to develop the skill of capturing, holding, and focusing the audience's attention until they have been absorbed into your world.

A state of captivation occurs when a person has lost connection with the real world and is completely wrapped up in what you are saying. This is what you experience when you are fully engrossed in a movie at the theater.

You have created a bridge between you and your listener. You will meet them on their side and bring them to your side.

What captures this kind of attention?

- Something they passionately agree with you about (pro-life/pro-choice, handguns/ban handguns, etc.).
- Something controversial that creates a significantly attention-getting emotion in them (anything that causes emotion that is *not so great* to take attention away from your story . . . nor too dull so that they pay no attention).
- Peripheral things that have nothing to do with the actual later content of the story (the camera focuses on the cheerleaders between plays to hold attention in commercial breaks).
- The setting or environment: where the story is being told (the restaurant you are in) . . . or if you are good . . . where the story takes place in the mind of the person you are talking to.

Imagine you and I are having a conversation, and you need to persuade me. You ask yourself, "What grabs Robert's attention about me?" Or "What am I trying to influence him to do or think?"

You want to wake up your listener. Meet them in their world, then walk them out of that world and bring them into a shared reality.

You meet the girl at the club. You have her tell her story about something that's really important to her. Perhaps it's a story about getting the new puppy she mentioned. The emotions she now feels as she tells the story are all positive, and the person she's connecting her puppy with now is you. When she has completely finished her tale you can then take her to a place in your past where you did something similar but not as impressive as what she did.

It's very important not to "one up" the other person. What matters is revealing a facet of identification.

"When I got my dog five years ago, I went to the pet store. It never dawned on me to go to the shelter and actually save an animal who then becomes your best friend because you saved them from being destroyed. I wish I had done that. But I have to say, I do love my dog. Did you see *Person of Interest* the other day? Great episode where Mr. Reese gives commands to what must have been his dog, and the dog saved his life because Mr. Reese was literally able to speak the language of the military dog. I've wanted to watch it again on TiVo. You gotta come over on Friday night and let's do that. Do you want to bring Pumpkin with you?"

1. We started in their world.
2. We met them in their world.
3. You walked them into your world.
4. You created a future shared reality.

32 | The Hidden Message

Each story you tell can have one hidden message that is potentially acceptable by the other person without conscious criticism.

If you want someone to know that you value loyalty or that you believe in God or someone found you to be smart, attractive, or a great lover, you want to pick one subtle message and stick with that message.

Avoid loading too much information into any one story. A good story maxes out at about four minutes in conversation when you're with one person. You get to tell one of those about every half hour. With small groups, you have to make your stories tighter and more concise. With large groups, of say 50 or more, you can tell a longer story if it is emotion-filled or action-packed. In that situation you could stretch to perhaps six to seven minutes but never more.

You embed hidden messages by using the exact words that someone else used in reference to you.

"And then her boyfriend yelled at her and said, 'what is he, a better lover than I am?'" Then she said, "It's like he wrote the book."

The quotes are positioned inside a story that could be about anything. The sentences have to comfortably fit the context, and they need to be real memories, or your nonconscious brain will betray you and tell the story differently each time, making the outcome you desire unpredictable.

Return the words that praise you to the lips of the people who originally spoke them. If you want them to know how bright you are, you will make sure the story you tell is one where *someone else* indicates your brilliance.

This is the beauty of subtle and hidden messages. It's why a testimonial means so much more to the average person than a scientific study.

And a testimonial that is singular in its message is always more effective than a testimonial that says you are smart, good looking, and a good gardener.

There is an even more elegant way to use hidden messages, revealing layers of meaning. You probably know them as "fables."

As an example, here is a pair of Ant and Grasshopper stories, one traditional and one updated, which you can use with different groups. You'll know which!

Ant and Grasshopper

Old Version

The ant works hard in the withering heat all summer long, building his house and laying up supplies for the winter.

The grasshopper thinks the ant is a fool and laughs and dances, has fun, and plays the summer away.

Come winter, the ant is warm and well-fed.

The grasshopper has no food or shelter, *so he dies out in the cold.*

MORAL OF THE STORY: Use your Conscious and Intentional Will Power and be responsible for yourself!

Updated Version

The ant works hard in the withering heat all summer long, building his house and laying up supplies for the winter.

The grasshopper thinks the ant is a fool and laughs and dances and plays the summer away.

Come winter, the shivering grasshopper calls a press conference and demands to know why the ant should be warm and well fed while all the grasshoppers are cold and starving.

CBS, NBC, FOX, PBS, CNN, and ABC show up to provide pictures of the shivering grasshopper next to a video of the ant in his comfortable home with a table filled with food. The world is stunned and appalled by the inequity and injustice . . . after all, a picture is worth a thousand words.

How can this be, that in a country of such wealth, this poor grasshopper is allowed to suffer so?

The ant is sent away, banished to never return.

The story ends as we see the grasshopper finishing up the last bits of the ant's food while the government house he is in, which just happens to be the ant's old house, crumbles around him because he doesn't maintain it . . . duh . . . he's a grasshopper.

BE AN ANT.

Use your choice of will.

33 | Psychic Power

Pain and fear are the two things people will do almost anything to avoid. The fight-or-flight response is a powerful one.

"Right now you're skeptical, and you should be. I would be, too."

How can you be so sure your future client is skeptical? Because they are human. We all tend to think and feel similar thoughts in certain contexts. When someone is trying to influence you, you put up defenses to protect yourself.

Most people think that by being quiet and saying very little their innermost thoughts are kept secret from you and the rest of the world. The fact of the matter is you can pretty much tell the person what is on their mind right now.

For example, I'm sitting across from you and for whatever reason you're not being real communicative with me. There are about a dozen different ways I can literally say something that appears to read your mind.

The context will determine what specific thought you will reveal. This is about as dramatic as you can get in subtly convincing someone of your capabilities.

Each of the simple phrases or sentence fragments below demonstrates how to use the most sure-fire mind-reading frames in existence.

"Hey man, you've suffered a lot of pain . . . it only makes sense to. . . . "

"I know you have concerns about the money. . . . "

"I have this sense that you are concerned about someone you love (care about) . . . maybe you're not worried but maybe you are. What's up?"

"Look, I know you want to change, but you hesitate because. . . ."

"Obviously, you're concerned about your appearance. I know that...."

"It's clear that you are feeling overwhelmed. You're working harder than ever at something, if not everything ... I want you to let us take care of...."

"I bet you are giving serious thought to making a change in how your income is earned, but you are concerned it will cost you. So you hesitate. But why?"

"I sense there is a lot of tension in part of your family. Someone you live with?"

When using the practiced techniques of mind-reading, people are more likely to listen to you, read your copy, listen to your presentation, to buy your product, and say yes to you. When you are making a direct connection to your customer's mind—their pain, their tension, their stress, their worries—you can momentarily highlight their pain, and then fix it for them.

34 | Bond Quickly

Several studies have revealed the very real fact that gossip acts as human glue.

If you are a man, you are probably venturing into somewhat uncharted territory here. Men don't make the best gossipers, for various biological and evolutionary reasons. But there is much to learn from the bond that women have. This shared experience is one of the key reasons culture has evolved in a way men don't understand.

Gossip would have you say something critical, disparaging, mean, unkind, nasty . . . about some other person.

Alicia and Beyonce have a meeting. Alicia's best chance to get Beyonce to join her cause, buy her product, or do just about anything, is to share something negative about Caitlin and have that something reciprocated.

Caitlin becomes the glue in a very close bond between Alicia and Beyonce.

This is how people become magnets to one and another.

It feels wrong. I don't like gossip. But it's simply the most common way people bond.

If you modify gossip into a technique, the criticism doesn't have to be all encompassing. It could be, but all it has to be is, "She can be such a bit*h . . . when things aren't going just perfect between her and Darryl."

The magnetism that is now felt between the two people is stronger than any other rapid link that can happen between two people, second only to sexual attraction. They are "friends at first sight," or more accurately, first criticism.

Gossip that causes the revelation of a shared negative attitude generates a friendship (bond).

Gossip isn't the only binder between two people. Sadly, however, it's the most effective.

Cavemen and women almost certainly gossiped and bonded. Gossip is a human characteristic that has bound people as long as language has been spoken. Gossip is typically about someone who is a threat of some kind to the gossiper.

Gossip seems harsh. But it has a huge evolutionary purpose. You have probably heard all of your friends gossiping about each other when that person is not in the group tonight. And they all still go to the party together next week.

I observe it literally every day.

Gossip isn't just a shared attitude; it's a shared attitude about someone else. It isn't positive. Sadly, positive attitudes are not as binding (between people) as negative attitudes and comments.

Gossip can be about many different people, close or distant to the teller.

The most popular celebrities are, by far, those that are gossiped about the most often: Kim Kardashian, Lindsay Lohan, Jessica Simpson, and Britney Spears. Women will generally tell you all kinds of interesting information about any of these four women. They comment on their weight, whether they've had surgery, whether they drink a lot of alcohol, have common sense, are famous only for being famous, or have no talent whatsoever.

Not bad for four multi-millionaire marketers, whose success is almost unparalleled in the United States. A big part of the reason for that success is because people gossip about them a great deal.

The gossip target could be an actress, the neighbor girl, the ex-boyfriend. The content could be anything that is negative enough to generate an emotional reaction in someone. It's gossip.

It's not necessary for Alicia and Beyonce to even know Caitlin, so long as they share the same criticism.

Shared Attitude Gossip

I can't recommend you gossip about people. It's difficult to even speak of it, but only a fool ignores the most powerful bonding tool in humanity.

There is a slightly less effective but still valuable tool you can use in place of people gossip.

A shared attitude about a hot button topic or a very polarizing religious or political opinion can accomplish similar results.

You aren't saying you saw the President grab a smoke; you're going to talk about one of his policies.

You don't know the President. I don't know the President.

From a bonding point of view, it is unwise to criticize someone with a sweeping generalization. If you're going to communicate with someone you are building rapport with, it is much smarter to talk about a specific trait, issue, belief, or policy.

The people who say "Never talk about religion or politics" are generally broke.

Subject Gossip is different than Object Gossip because the person might like the other person but feel hostile toward a single idea they hold.

What about positive stuff?

Dan is talking to Edward and says, "Hey, you like The Beatles, too?"

That is like the kid's paste that is on the other end of the spectrum of Super Glue. It's a step in a direction where the gossip is the Super Glue.

Why?

When you find out that someone likes something, they had that on their wall. It's like advertising. The guy at the office puts a picture of his fishing trip in plain sight. You see that, but you really haven't made a huge discovery. It's there; it's just generally not huge. There are exceptions when the piece recognized is about mutually shared identities.

But people don't typically put their negative attitudes and beliefs up on the wall for everyone to see. When you discover this guy doesn't like something about someone, you've made a real discovery. You've learned *more* about them than you did discovering a positively held view.

Let's get crystal clear.

Discovery is key, and stealth is necessary

Once you find out someone else is disgusted with *X*, if you also share that disgust, you have a powerful connection. How strong? People can live with each other for 10 years and not have a connection so binding.

Familiarity Is a Magnet

People who share a negatively held attitude toward another become closer because the shared negative attitude makes them *familiar* to each other. It also creates "We" against "Them."

When you hear people gossiping, realize that you don't have to join in. In fact you probably shouldn't. But also realize that they are gossiping. That means the Super Glue is bonding.

35 | Use a Post-It® Note

Post-it notes are goofy and they don't blend into the environment in any way. They get in your face.

But a Post-it note gets attention and it gets priority.

The Post-it note influences.

Randy Garner of Sam Houston State University (Huntsville) did a brilliant series of studies on Post-it notes and just how influential they are.

Garner knows that marketers and salespeople need people to act. You need people to do stuff you want them to do *now*. Getting people to comply with anything that requires effort is extremely valuable to you and me.

Thanks to him, we can find out whether a simple Post-it note . . . with nothing written on it . . . influences.

Study 1: Does the Post-It Note Really Influence?

In one study, he sent surveys by mail to a group of 150 professors. They would receive the following:

Group 1: A survey, with a Post-it note attached, asking for the return of the completed survey.
Group 2: A survey, with the same handwritten message added to a standard cover letter, instead of an attached Post-it note.
Group 3: A survey, with a cover letter, but no handwritten message.

What happened?

Group 1 recipients returned the completed survey in 76 percent of cases.
Group 2 recipients returned the completed survey in 48 percent of cases.
Group 3 recipients returned the completed survey in 36 percent of cases.

For a number of reasons, the Post-it note is almost magic. Garner nailed it before anyone else.

Please understand exactly *why* the Post-it note works so well. It represents *many* powerful behavioral triggers all in one little object.

It doesn't match the environment. The brain hates it.
It gets attention first because of #1.
It is **personalized** (the difference between Group 2 and Group 3).
It is personalized to the point of an afterthought (the difference between 1 and 2).

Ultimately, it associates **one person** communicating with **another important person**—almost as if it is a favor or special request.

36

More Post-It® Magic

Garner found the gold mine and then tested to see if there is actual magic in the Post-it note.

He's going to send a group in Study 2 a **blank** Post-it note attached to surveys sent to one of the groups.

Here's what they received:

Group 1: A survey with a **message** on a Post-it note.
Group 2: A survey with a **blank** Post-it note attached.
Group 3: A survey with **no** Post-it note.

Now what happens in this second study?

Group 1: 69 percent completed and returned their survey (roughly the same response as Group 1 in the first study).
Group 2: 43 percent completed and returned their survey (received with a blank Post-it note).
Group 3: 34 percent completed and returned their survey (no Post-it note).

There might be a little magic in the actual Post-it note, but the reality is . . . probably not. This is about **Identity**. The person sending the survey is personally asking me in a special way (not just writing it on the survey) to help him out.

Dr. Garner could easily have stopped here, but there is more to this than Ultimate Compliance.

Study 3: Does the Post-It Note Influence Speed of Compliance?

Garner now wanted to examine how promptly people would return a follow-up survey if there was a Post-it note attached and how **much** information the person being surveyed would return with that Post-it note, compared to those who did not receive an attached Post-it note.

> Group 1: (Post-it note attached) 64 percent returned the packet.
> Group 2: (No Post-it) 42 percent returned the packet. (Results similar to Study 2 Group 3.)

> Group 1 returned their survey in an average of about four days.
> Group 2 returned their survey in an average of about five and a half days.

And . . .

Group 1 sent significantly more comments and answered more open-ended questions with more words than did Group 2.

That's where most university research stops.

What makes Garner's work special is that he wants to demonstrate whether this only aids compliance in simpler requests, or if the effect carries to more involved tasks.

Do Personalized Notes Influence People?

Study 4: Does a Personalized Post-It Note Create Even More Magic?

This time, Garner sends 90 participants a long survey and 90 a short survey (half the size).

Each group was divided into three smaller groups.

Group A received a Post-it note request.

Group B received a personalized Post-it note request with the individual's name on it as well as "Thank you" and Garner's initials at the bottom of the sticky note.

Group C received no Post-it note.

What happened?

Post-It Note versus Personalized Note versus No Note

Long Version: 40 percent versus 67 percent versus 13 percent

Short Version: 70 percent versus 77 percent versus 33 percent

It appears that if the task is simple, the simple Post-it note request needs no further personalization. The effect is strong and significant in both experimental conditions.

But when the task is more involved, the personalized note was significantly more effective than the simple standard Post-it note request.

37 | Seven New Body Language Tips

Here's a selection of key body language movements to help the other person feel connected to you and, at the same time, lower their defenses.

1. Quickly assess their speed of communication, body gestures, and even their general walking speed if you have the opportunity to observe them. You'll roughly synchronize their life pace and it will bring the two of you onto the same page ... at the same time.
2. Do not smile unless it really makes sense to do so. A fake smile is easy to decode and comes across as untrustworthy.
3. Do not move into the personal space of another. Their side of the table is theirs, unless they invite you in by first straying into yours.
4. Do not touch your hands to your face. It is never perceived as professional or attractive and can indicate deception.
5. Do not scratch anything ... ever. Again, it can indicate deception and it's only an itch!
6. Your hands (which should already be clean and with nails clean and trimmed short) should not touch each other. The big signal you want to preclude is "going in for the kill." The other is nervousness.
7. Keep your feet pointed toward the person you are talking to. Pointing away is seen as an unconscious indicator you want to run away.

38 | Triggering Feelings of Inclusion

There *is* a place for praise and flattery. It is especially effective to use questions to indicate your praise.

"How did you become so good at doing this?"

"Why do other people seem to have such difficulty? You make that look easy; how did you get so good at this?"

By asking questions that praise the other person, you can dramatically lower defenses, allowing your suggestions to slip by any normal scrutiny and be accepted more easily and quickly.

When I was a kid, I'd tell my grandmother she looked "real nice" before we would go to church. She consistently replied, "Flattery will get you everywhere, Number One Son."

I actually had no agenda beyond letting my grandmother know she looked nice and wanting her to feel good about knowing that she did.

Praise sails right past our usual critical faculty, causing people to come together in agreement and enhancing their willingness to comply with requests without the usual scrutiny.

39 | Regret Reduction

No matter how much people need to make a decision to relieve pain, and no matter how much relief they might get, they will inevitably feel some remorse once the deed is done. They will feel regret even when it's not logical.

Some people feel regret when they break off the old relationship and commit to the new one. It's only natural. The choice has been eliminated, for now, and choice elimination, while an ingredient for influence, can also cause feelings of freedom being restricted.

People often feel regret when they open the package and it's not what they expected to see.

They also often regret owning the new car on day three. They get to thinking about the finances and all the repercussions of having a new vehicle.

People sometimes experience regret right when they get home with the product.

Regret, and even the anticipation of regret, is a big problem you face when influencing others.

There are a few consistent methods of overcoming regret, depending on the context, of course:

- With involvement
- With something that feels/looks really good
- With a reminder of their good decision to buy

Involvement in the persuasion process is one method to quell regret. In direct mail, you've seen the pieces where you receive stamps, stickers, and things you have to tear out, lick, or put into place on an order form. Once you've spent time (been involved) in making an order, you are more committed to the order.

The more involved the other person, the less likely they are to revert to the status quo.

Many marketers put a card inside of products that urge the customer to call a 1-800 phone number to register for the teleseminars that relate to the product. The person on the line would ask the customer questions such as "How was your product received? Was everything in the package? How did it look?" The questions are designed to remind them of how fabulous the program looks and feels, and how excited they will be when they use it.

You can send a reminder after the purchase that congratulates the customer on making such a great purchase. Remind them how good they felt upon buying, bring back those good feelings, and chase away the buyer's remorse they may have otherwise felt.

40

"I can't afford it."

Here's what to do when you hear that almost instinctive reaction to most offers, which is either "No," or "Not now," or "Later." They all seem like reasonable and safe responses because they protect the person from getting hurt or being otherwise negatively impacted if they make a bad choice.

However, if you use this phrase you can open doors to a new level of thought.

It might sound like this:

Employee: "I can't afford to open a 401(k)!"

Manager: "That's exactly why you should. You need to pay yourself something. At the moment you're working to pay the mortgage lender, the banks, the car dealership, the IRS, and what's left over for you? You're worth something."

Or this:

Dan: "Cool smartphone! I can't afford one of those."

Jason: "That's probably why you should get one. How are you keeping in contact with clients when you're not at your computer? It always takes ages for you to get back by e-mail when you're out of the office, so how much business are you losing? It would be much cheaper than buying an iPad to take around with you."

Phil: "I can't afford to have my lawn aerated."

Lawn service: "That's exactly why you should pay us to do that. You'll save yourself the cost of re-sodding the entire lawn next year if you do."

There is a lot going on in those exchanges but consider the highlights:

- They use the concern as the new frame for **why they should** buy now.
- A new piece of potentially face-saving information is presented. So if the person is "proud," they can say "Oh, I didn't realize there was 0 percent financing available." This allows them to agree and still maintain their pride.
- They present information in a startling way by actually disagreeing with them. Most people would have agreed with them or taken them at their word.

41 Put It on Paper

There are many times when you want people you are communicating with to take notes. They might not want to, but see if you can get them to take handwritten notes or use their computer. The aim is to get them to expose their concerns faster.

The first thing is to have them write all the details and benefits you describe in your proposal on the left-hand side of the page. On the right they are invited to provide *their own* counter examples or objections to what you are proposing. You let them know that as soon as they have a concern, an objection, or a disagreement, they need to write it down in the right-hand column.

Once they have written everything down, it cements the fact that you are important enough for them to have recorded what you said. (Who else did you ever take notes from?) Additionally, no one was expecting you to *want* to hear all their arguments against your proposal.

The act of writing the two columns puts them in a position of comparing both sides of the situation. They're most likely to notice that the left-hand side of the paper holds 97 percent of the written text, and theirs has only 3 percent. Therefore, you must be pretty smart.

At the end of a note-taking session in a group setting, you can ask for volunteers to come to the front if their concern has still not been dealt with. The more you validate, the more confident you appear.

This exercise also provides a dramatic comparison of how little people actually disagree with you when they write all their concerns down and see them on paper.

42 | Choice Sequencing

Roberto Monaco came, along with his thick Brazilian accent, to *Influence: Boot Camp* in Vegas. He ended up making millions of dollars for this nation's best known motivational speaker by employing a well-presented choice strategy.

Here's how he explained what I taught him to subsequent students at the annual event:

"I want you guys to write down three numbers:

- $2,497
- $1,297
- $997

"A long time ago, back in 2006, I was selling this speaker's event, and the way we were positioning our offering was to have the best package at $2,497 and the second package, VIP level, at $1,297. Then the Executive package at $997 which was the last thing I talked about.

"Most people bought the $997, so we came to *Influence: Boot Camp* and I explained this problem to Kevin in front of everybody. Fun group, you're learning, taking notes. I had my boss there, the head of sales, and I just showed this to Kevin.

"Kevin said, 'I have an idea for you. Which one has the most value for people?'

"I told Kevin, 'The $1,297 because the $2,497 is out of range for most people. You want to sell more of the $1,297.'

"Kevin said, 'Here is how you do it. Start on the top $2,497, go all the way down to the $997, and where you really spend time, the last thing you talk about, is the $1,297. You circle that on the whiteboard, and you talk about how and precisely why it is an excellent value.'"

Roberto then told the audience at Boot Camp, "Really, that's kind of awkward; I start on the top, go to the bottom, and back in the middle, kind of weird. Personally I started doing that because Kevin told us to do it. But my closing conversion rate of the $1,297 went up over 40 percent overall. Then I taught the guys with my team and they experienced an overall 30 percent increase. That little two-minute strategy that this man, Kevin Hogan, showed us has made millions and millions of sales in seminars. So much so that we named it 'The Kevin Hogan Close.' You became very famous, Kevin. It's really, really powerful."

(Roberto is co-founder of www.influenceology.com.)

43 | Generate This Specific Sequence of Emotions

The three examples that follow illustrate the combinations of emotions most likely to succeed at generating compliance.

Imagine you're crossing a street but *not* in the crosswalk at the intersection.

All of a sudden a whistle blows! It must be a policeman. Your heart pounds as you wonder if it's about you and how much trouble you are in for jaywalking. This kind of experience immediately changes your state from goal-oriented behavior (crossing the street) to one of a state of fear and guilt.

You look around and, seeing no police, you continue across the street. You are immediately stopped by someone. You again think you could be in trouble. More fear pulsates through your body.

He says, "Excuse me. I need 10 minutes of your time to answer a few questions for me. It's the Self Description Inventory. . . ."

In this first study, a bunch of people were randomly stopped, after hearing the whistle on this cold day in Poland, by Dariusz Dolinski's group of researchers. Another bunch of people were stopped as well, but they crossed **without** hearing the whistle.[1]

---

[1] D. Dolinski and K. Szczucka, "See Saw of Emotions and Compliance," *Journal of Experimental Social Psychology* 34 (2008): 27–50.

Finally, a third group of people were stopped as well as they walked along the sidewalk. No jaywalking and no whistle. They were just walking along.

What happened?

- 59 percent of the people who heard the whistle while jaywalking agreed to fill out the survey.
- 46 percent of the jaywalkers who heard no whistle agreed as well.
- 41 percent of those on an evening stroll on the cold day agreed to answer questions.

So people were **more** compliant when they were caught doing something wrong, albeit very small.

In a second study, experimenters found illegally parked cars and placed leaflets that **looked like tickets** on the windshield under the wiper. (They were actually either requests for blood donation or hair restoring shampoo promotions.)

The experimenters also taped the leaflets to the door handles of other cars. (Not indicative of a ticket, something you would **feel** much different about, right?)

Finally, there was a group of cars that were illegally parked, and nothing was done.

As each person returned to their car and was about to leave, an experimenter approached and asked the driver to give them a few minutes for a quick survey for his master's thesis on *Efficient Traffic*.

So who complied with the request for a quick survey?

- 57 percent of those with a potential ticket (shampoo ad) under the wiper.
- 68 percent of those with a potential ticket (appeal for blood donation).
- 34 percent of those with a shampoo ad leaflet taped to the car door.
- 40 percent of those with a blood donation leaflet taped to the car door.
- 36 percent of those who were only illegally parked and received no leaflet.

By inducing **fear and guilt**, and then offering relief, the researchers almost doubled the subjects' compliance.

Our third example is an experiment carried out to test whether people comply because of **fear only** or because they experienced **fear** followed by the **relief of fear**.

Students at a university were divided into three rooms:

Room 1: Participants experienced electric shocks for misspelled words. (Fear.)

Room 2: Participants experienced electric shocks for misspelled words, but were then told to go into the hall where they were reassigned to a dart throwing experiment. (Fear, then relief.)

Room 3: Students were asked to throw darts from various distances. (Nothing or Control Group.)

Outside all the rooms, following the experimental activity, a female student approached students in the hall, one by one, asking for participation in a charity event for an orphanage. Students were asked how much time they would volunteer at the event.

The results were as follows:

Room 1: (Fear) 37 percent complied, promising an average of five hours.
Room 2: (Fear, then relief) 75 percent complied, promising an average of nine hours.
Room 3: (Control) 52 percent complied, promising an average of eight hours.

The induction and then *reduction* of fear causes compliance in requests immediately following the emotional seesaw drama. As you can see, the result is highly significant and much more so than simply creating fear.

44

The Instant
Drama Resolution
Technique

Closely related to the previous technique, these experiments reveal that other emotions, aside from fear and relief, can increase compliance. Read each to see how you could tailor this to your situation(s).

Happiness Followed by Disappointment

The first experiment that Narwat and Dolinski did to test this was on the streets of Wroclaw, Poland.[1] (As I recall, that is pronounced roughly, Frahtswahf!)

People would see what looked like a 50 zloty ($15) bill on the sidewalk and pick it up. It wasn't. It only looked like money. It was an ad for a new car wash.

Most people threw the ad in the garbage. (I was impressed!)

Soon after, a female confederate appeared with a suitcase that needed to be watched: "I urgently have to see my friend who is on the fifth floor in the building here, and my bag is too heavy!"

---

[1] R. Narwat and D. Dolinski, "'Fear-Then-Relief' Procedure for Producing Compliance: Beware When the Danger Is Over," *Journal of Experimental Social Psychology* 34, no. 1 (January 1998): 27–50.

The key result was that the people who had picked up the "money" (really the car wash ad) were **twice as likely** to watch the bag for the girl as those people who found nothing on the street!

What?! Wait just a minute.

Someone is superexcited to find what looks like money. Then they find out it's just a stupid car wash ad. Then they are asked to watch a piece of heavy luggage for a girl, and these people are **twice as likely** to do so as people who found nothing?! *What?*

In a related experiment, German students in one group were told they received an A on a test, and then were told they truly received a C. The professor had made a mistake.

In another group the students were told they received a C on the test and then it was corrected, that they actually received an A.

In yet another group the students were given the accurate grade they received on the test.

Students were then informed that there would be a street party next quarter, and the school was looking for volunteers to have an information booth and to help prepare cake and coffee.

Students were asked to commit to a number of hours they would work on that Sunday and write it down. Here's what happened:

- Negative feelings—C then positive A: They offered three hours.
- Positive then negative—A then C: They offered two hours.
- Positive (correct score): They offered 1.1 hours.
- Control (no info): They offered 1.2 hours.

In the two nondrama situations, where they were given the correct score or there was no information provided, the student offered the minimum one hour of volunteering. But when there is emotional drama, things change fast . . . and significantly.

According to Dariusz Dolinski, "the withdrawal of emotions is an effective instrument of social influence that works no matter whether the participants first experienced disappointment and dissatisfaction then happiness and the sense of well-being, or whether the sequence is reversed. . . . The fast change in the emotional quality leads to increased compliance."

45 | Cause Them to Be Interrupted

Interruption, like brief confusion, can be the beginning of change. When people begin talking about something, particularly if there is a sale to be made, the potential customer is in one particular frame of mind (good or bad, analyzing or salivating) when the conversation begins; when an interruption occurs, that **frame** is gone.

You're in a meeting with three other people. Someone bursts into the office and brings up something completely unrelated to the subject at hand. They finally leave. After the interruption, you may have a completely different mind-set—and make a completely different decision.

Last week I was going shopping and I wanted to get something cool at Hallmark. I arrived and the store was closed. I couldn't believe it. But there it was with a sign saying their holiday hours were *shortened*!

So I got back in the car and went over to Target.

Essentially, I had made up my mind to spend X dollars at Y location, and I was interrupted and totally shifted gears, finally spending money with someone who wanted to let me buy something!

That's roughly the same as an interruption, but with one big difference. I had been in "analysis mode" on my way to Hallmark, thinking how much money to spend, what to get, how creative I might get. When I was "interrupted," my thinking changed. I went into "emotional mode" and was then driven by desires. That little change caused me to spend 10 to 15 times more money than I would have at Hallmark!

Research shows that when people are interrupted they don't resume the previous pattern of thinking. Instead of being focused on value or price, they now focus on what they want. They do indeed spend more money and spend it faster.

Write this down:

Preinterruption, people think Bottom Up, Detail Oriented, and Price Conscious. They are thinking price feasibility.

Postinterruption, people think Top Down. They become Goal Oriented. *Desires* become the key. Price feasibility is *not* what people are thinking about.

46 | Recapturing Attention

It's not unusual for events to occur while you are communicating with someone. We've talked about deliberately creating interruptions, but now let's talk about what to do with unwanted interruptions.

Perhaps you are about to ask someone out.

Perhaps you are about to ask for the big deal.

Perhaps you are two-thirds of the way through a critical presentation.

You are interrupted and it wasn't your intended interruption. At this point you must recapture attention.

Laurent Itti, University of Southern California, Pierre Baldi, University of California, Irvine discovered there are five factors that determine what captures our attention. They are:

1. Surprise location
2. Surprise observation
3. Surprise event
4. Salience (importance to you)
5. Entropy (message fading or randomness in moving experience)

There is a difference between who gets attention and who gets picked, but if you *do not* get attention, you *cannot* be picked!

You must recapture attention when it's been lost, and you don't have long to do it.

The scientific research showed that **surprise** is the most important factor in attention, followed by **salience** (importance to you) and **entropy** (unpredictability, randomness of events or experience).

Write that down. Tape it to your computer.

Always be prepared for the implementation of something surprising or remarkably salient to put you back in control of the discussion at hand.

47 | Decide Right Now

In a situation where further analysis and hesitation would be counterpro-
ductive, ask, "If you had to decide right now, in this minute, what would
you decide?" Then, get them to write the decision down. Then, walk away.
Go and do something else or talk about something else. Come back to the
decision after a short amount of time has passed and get them to read the
decision and see if they still agree. If so, go forward. If not, ask them to make
another decision and repeat this cycle.

"If you had to decide right now, in this minute, between getting model
A4 with the three-year warranty or model A5 with the one-year warranty,
which would you pick?"

A further reduction of choice to just one thing might look like this:

You and your client have spent around four hours up to this point in
your discussions about whether to develop an ongoing relationship. You're
eager to close, so you ask, "Okay, do you think you're ready to go ahead
with this plan?" If the answer is not positive, you ask, "So, what's the **one**
thing you need to get fixed in order for this to work?"

48

Generate an Irresistible Impulse

There are many unexpected triggers that can cause impulsive behavior.

One of my favorite generators of impulsive behavior is the Reward Card or Loyalty Program.

I fly Delta. Delta is an airline with high prices. They are an airline that charges for every piece of Kleenex used. But Delta has a hub in the city I live in. I can get to most places without having to make a stop. The alternative to Delta is flying other airlines that are likely to stop on a lot of their routes.

Three years ago I was one flight away from being Platinum, instead of Gold, for the following year. It was December. I booked a flight to Las Vegas for a quick turnaround trip and accumulated enough miles to "put me over the top." Now I'm Platinum.

Platinum sounds cool.

Platinum fliers get lots of upgrades to first class from coach and certainly a lot more upgrades than Gold fliers.

But was it really worth the time and money and effort?

Platinum members will generally tell you yes, though it is mostly an emotional decision and certainly one that has some push behind it.

Restaurants and car washes often wisely use reward systems, but frankly most don't know the science behind the approach so they generally fail.

If you understand the psychology behind the correct use of loyalty and reward, you can implement the method in your business and you can implement it in your personal life as well.

It turns out there is a big difference in whether or not a rewards card using stamps gives you a head start by crediting the buyer of a car wash with three stamps (purchases) when they are first given the card, filling 3 of 12 slots, compared to a card that simply had 9 purchases to go before a free car wash could be obtained.

Both, of course, required nine additional purchases, the only difference was the total amount of spaces, 9 versus 12, and the spaces already stamped, 0 versus 3. That's it. **The latter generated multiple amounts of sales and revenues.**

The success of this strategy has nothing to do with language or answering objections. It's not whether the card will be effective: it's the function of the card that causes an **irresistible impulse to complete** the card.

If you have 3 out of 10 of something and need seven more before you can "cash it in," it's pretty compelling. No one likes to leave money on the table.

If you have 0 out of 10 spaces stamped . . . there is no compulsion and nothing that hurts if you leave it on the table.

You'd get upset if someone threw away the card that had seven spaces stamped.

Think about it.

But if you had another card, or even 10 cards with one stamp on each and someone threw them away, you'd pay no attention. You wouldn't care. Oh, and you wouldn't be a customer . . . certainly not as often.

By placing the right things in people's hands, you cause very different results. But it's not just the right things. It's making sure that they are placed there and then used in a psychologically calculated fashion. Only one combination turns the tumblers to open the safe.

One specific way creates a thriving business; try the others and the doors close. The cost is zero, the implementation cost is zero, but the differences in results are dramatic.

And by the way, the phenomenon itself isn't about reward cards. It's about a lot more than the **one** manifestation of a principle, right?

It's about the irresistible impulse. The **nagging compulsion to complete.**

Involve the other person in an activity that they will feel compelled to complete; otherwise, they will experience that sense of loss of having left, perhaps, money on the table or the equivalent thereof.

49

Take Them
for a Walk

Here's one I've never shared.

It's very difficult for someone to say no when you use this approach.

Quite often your suggestion or request will engender resistance because the proposed action is difficult to do.

For example, agreeing to take an extra $100 out of their paycheck each week to put in their retirement account isn't the no-brainer you and I know it should be.

Another example is suggesting that they replace one or two snacks each day with a salad or a piece of fruit. It seems like a smart idea but the person immediately resists the message, knowing how they feel about their chocolate fixes.

Another example is agreeing to daily exercise that exceeds what they have done in the past.

Perhaps you're asking them to cut the lawn for you for the next few weeks.

Other proposals that are difficult include anything that requires their sustained effort over time.

Whenever your proposal implies or explicitly states that the other person might have to work at something they are unfamiliar with, or have not done before, you induce discomfort. If you ask them to do something they typically don't do, you probably need them to comply for the sake of their health, their wealth, or the benefit of their family. But they are indeed very resistant.

At this point, you can improve the likelihood of having your proposal accepted by using psychological distancing.

If you have a brochure for a new home gym you want them to see, you do not want to place it in their hands. Instead you might want to display it on your side of the table, not theirs. The actual physical distance to the object inducing anxiety is farther away, outside of their personal space, and that distance, while very small, will create a more receptive attitude in the individual.

If you want them to sign on the dotted line to increase their retirement savings, you might want to place the agreement at arm's length from them and next to other innocuous papers that create no resistance for them.

If the person is sitting in a chair that reclines, you can literally ask them to sit back and relax while you do the work in presenting the information.

All of these subtle shifts in physical distance cause resistance to be reduced in an individual who is expecting any actions required of him to be difficult in some way.

The brain's wiring requires the body to move away from that which causes anxiety. You can physically walk someone to a different location. You can ask them to think about how they would look on that side of the house "over there."

Talking while you take a walk can be an excellent way to gain agreement on tasks that have to be done at the house.

Perhaps you need to persuade your partner to help you paint the deck. The place to ask for that help is probably not **on** the deck if they are going to find the project to be a lot of work and very undesirable. However, the same conversation on the walk provides a significant physical and psychological distance from the problem.

Take people for a walk or have them sit farther back from the front of the room. It will often be the difference between yes and no.

50

The Story and the Statistic

The national debt of the United States of America is 16 trillion dollars, as of this writing. That, in and of itself, doesn't mean anything. Compare that to the Gross Domestic Product of the United States (the sum of all the final product stuff we produce in the United States), which is also right around 16 trillion dollars.

That means that America is in debt to the tune of what its gross sales are.

That's pretty scary . . . if you know statistics . . .

Then there's another fact:

The United States collects about $2 trillion in taxes every year. So our debt is eight times our income.

Finally, we spend $3.5 trillion per year, so we are adding $1.5 trillion to the national debt each year.

That certainly sounds like it must be bad. That's probably something that someone should look into and work on, right? That's something that probably needs fixing. But it doesn't keep you up at night.

Now contrast **that** with **this**:

"Imagine your family, which earns $80,000 per year, was in debt by $640,000. Imagine that each year that $640,000 increased by another $50,000. I have a question. What would be happening in your life right now?"

"We'd have to file for bankruptcy."

"Why?"

"Because our payments would be $130,000 per year, our income would only be $80,000, and the bank would foreclose on the house because we couldn't make payments. We'd have to give up the home, and we'd owe more than we could ever pay for. Might as well just all go jump in the river."

"What your country is doing is even worse to you and your kids. They owe all that money, and what has to happen is that the people to whom the money is owed, well, they aren't going to get it because there is nothing to pay them with. Pretty quick here, retirees who invested in conservative government bonds will be out of retirement money because those bonds will be worthless. The government won't make the payments. The countries who have loaned us money will start moving in because we have no money to pay them back. The money you have will be nothing more than pieces of paper when you go to the grocery store, which now only accepts gold and silver. Your kids' college education won't matter because there will be no college—there will be no way to pay teachers, or utility workers, or gas stations, or grocery stores. Essentially, when money becomes worthless, it's going to get pretty ugly. After all, how would you get food? How would you heat your house? There would be no electricity or water flowing because there would be no more money. How would your kids live in such a place?"

Statistics are crystal clear to people who think in terms of numbers and are able to do mathematical calculations. But the *story* is what really brings the problem home. The story is compelling. It demands that something be done.

Statistics, as every politician knows, simply don't convince because people don't understand numbers. But they do understand stories.

Stories keep you up at night. . . .

51 | Understanding, and the Alternative

Influence often comes down to someone deciding to do or not do something based upon how they feel *now*, regardless of what might happen in the future.

In this moment, feelings carry a lot more weight in the brain than do images of future possibilities.

Therefore most people will say no to most proposals where something good in the future is pitted against something in the present.

If you were to say to someone, "This $500 advertisement should bring in $5,000 for your business over the next year. Sound good?" the answer is generally "No."

The good news is you'll never again have to make that kind of an offer to your prospective client.

Instead, you are going to have them get into a different frame of mind. They are shortly going to be processing information in such a way that peripheral feelings are not considered, and only the options presented are evaluated.

"That's it. You could take the big screen plasma home and never use it. The $1,000 investment easily could go unused. You could easily get busy and really rarely watch anything on TV. That's a very real possibility.

"It's also possible that you could put that $1,000 out there, have a beautiful 50" plasma TV and watch it an hour or so each day. Your favorite shows. *Big Bang Theory, Person of Interest,* football, *Two Broke Girls, Survivor, Revolution, The Apprentice, The Last Resort,* and on and on. It's really 100 percent your decision. Do what you want to do."

Contrast the person's feared reality with the more likely reality. Offer the likely reality last.

52 | Give Them Meaning

Each day people go to work at the same place, doing the same thing, with the same people, getting the same results, going home the same route, and repeating it all over again tomorrow.

Familiarity certainly provides comfort, but the repetitive life can also create a loss of meaning.

Humans have need for meaning in their life.

They don't generally need meaning over and above the acquisition of comfort, familiarity, eating, a safe place to live, or reproducing.

But once those items are satisfied, life does need to have some meaning to it or the human mind begins to become dysfunctional.

When people tell you that what you are doing matters in life, it makes you feel something more than good. It makes you feel empowered. It gives you strength. It rejuvenates you, and it creates instant respect and liking from you for that person.

Giving someone meaning is not saying "You did a great job on that." (This is a comment specific to their effort.)

It's also not "You are so smart!" (This is specific to their attribute of intelligence.)

Viktor Frankl wrote that meaning is the *primary* motivational force in man.

M.I.T. researchers found what might be the two puzzle pieces that fit together to create the center of meaning. A series of experiments where people accomplished elementary tasks offered fascinating revelations.

Subjects would do mindless tasks longer and for less financial reward as long as another person was there to observe them finish their work.

Another finding was that if people could somehow show that the work accomplished was their own, say, by having their name on the sheet of paper, they would perform better.

When people's work was destroyed immediately upon completion, they ultimately didn't continue working as less money was offered. They also didn't complete as much work as people who got to put their name on their work.

Meaning, or the lack of it, is a part of our identity.

By suggesting to the other person that what they are doing matters, you connect with the person's desire for meaning in a way few others will. People need to know that their life matters.

Remind them.

A 10-Step Influence Template

Here's one simple template of influence you can use today. The details are left out so you can see the big picture. There are many templates, and this is just one, but it is pretty darned efficient and packs a big punch!

Foundation: Expectancy is at a level of the obvious. You have your most useful Self forward and you know "who" you want to talk to.

1. Determine and Control the Context

Mindsets: What the person is experiencing emotionally and what they have experienced that same day, or in similar situations in the past, will affect their decisions.

Places: People respond and react (unconsciously) very differently in different settings. Think of your behavior being different in a library, a hospital waiting room, a sports stadium, McDonald's, or an elegant restaurant.

People: We also react differently around different people, morphing some of their personality into ours and vice versa. So when you communicate with someone, who else is around who is going to influence your client's decision, other than you?

Things: If you are at the newsstand and you are standing next to someone reading *Time*, *Newsweek* (I think it is going straight digital now!), or *Bloomberg Businessweek*, in contrast to another person reading *Maxim* or *Esquire*, you have two different contexts that shift your mind-set.

All of the things in the environment, including your clothes, persuade. Everything matters. Everything triggers thoughts and feelings. Everything causes other things to happen inside that move you closer or further away from your objective.

Being able to control contextual and environmental variables to their most optimal level is dramatically important for successful influence.

2. Determine My Outcome

My desired outcome and my client's must be mutually beneficial. What specifically do I want to happen? What is my target? It's important to know what you want to result from your encounter. A satisfied customer or a loyal friend?

I will always want something productive to come out of a meeting or an engagement. I will want a value exchange. Whatever the case, I will generally determine my outcome prior to saying hello.

My outcome is much more than what I get out of a deal. My outcome is also going to include the other person getting what they need or want. In most situations I will have considered what will likely help someone, or a group, most and have a plan to accomplish my outcome.

If I can't help them get what they want, I don't want anything out of the deal. Never attempt to influence someone to where you end up with an imbalance. If you make $100 by selling $1,000,000 of value, that's fine. But if you get $100,000 in exchange for $20,000 of value, you won't sleep at night.

Be crystal clear on both sides of the equation walking in the door, so the other person doesn't have any reason to be resistant. Plan for them to do well and plan for them to invite you back next year.

3. Identify and Empathize

You can't influence if you don't have empathy. In most cases, the people I persuade become my friends. That's always my goal, and I generally succeed. I want to feel out who my client is and what their desires, drives, wants, and motivators are. More importantly, I want to know what they are experiencing in life right now. If they are going through particularly difficult times, that experience can leave them vulnerable to making a poor decision today. In situations like that, it's better to help them with the problem at hand and take care of your business with them at a different time, unless they suggest otherwise.

If you knew when someone was scared, distrusting, connected, distant, distracted, confident, or in denial, that could be a big advantage in selling and in marketing in general. There are appropriate times to utilize that knowledge to complete a deal, and there are times when you use that information to walk away until another day.

4. Defuse Resistance and Reactance

Reactance and resistance are normal experiences that occur in each communication. Expect them. Defuse major resistance by pointing out a flaw in yourself. I make fun of myself; I show imperfections in products. People don't go searching for what you've already shown them.

Reactance is that gut-level, genetic, automatic reaction to anything that in *any way* is going to attempt to influence a change to happen.

Any kind of change. *Any* kind of difference. *Anything* that isn't the way it is now.

Reactance is an evolutionary force that is designed to protect the person and the group from danger. And only after the person is absolutely certain at the gut level that things are safe, will they move beyond reactance.

I was reading some copy online the other day. I thought it was quite creative how the marketer defused resistance in his advertising copy.

He warns, "Only one of two things will happen when you order this product. Either A: You will get it and never open it. You might even return it—because you're lazy. You didn't do what was inside. Or B: You will get it, do it, and be successful! You will make a lot of money, and it will change your life."

The notion to put it all upfront essentially eliminates that gut-level reactance. What remains is resistance that is completely acceptable.

5. Defuse Feelings of Anticipated Regret

"If I buy this I'm going to regret it. . . . "

It's time to go back to the future. Here, you need to take people on a journey to the future and show how they could possibly regret their decision, but then paint the more likely scenario, which is that your product or service will give them what they want and need.

I might understandably have feelings of regret about buying things if I had bought something in the past and it just sat unused in the garage.

Take people out into the future; show them what could happen, what else could happen, and then what is most likely to actually occur.

You could even tell them the most extraordinary thing that could happen: "You could become a millionaire!" and then say, "But, what will probably happen is that you'll do fine, you'll utilize the information, and you'll make a few hundred thousand dollars, and everything will be okay." Exaggerating outcomes can go a long way toward people thinking in realistic terms and not having exaggerated hopes themselves.

6. Carefully Frame the Proposal

The mortality rate of surgery A is 20 percent. The chances of living through surgery B are 80 percent. Which surgery do you want to have? Of course B—except . . . they are the same! Yet the frame of one sentence costs people their lives every day. Think carefully of how you want to frame your proposal.

If I say, "20 percent of the people who pick up this new gardening tool will never open it," and if I don't say anything more, what will happen? They aren't going to be convinced that the garden tool is worthwhile.

However, I can say, "80 percent of the individuals who pick up this garden tool will utilize it to go on to massive success and wealth in their lives." This frame will likely get many more customers to pick up the program.

7. Propose a Solution

Propose a solution that might be the desired outcome. But first offer an alternative or two that are inferior for some almost obvious reason, such as too expensive or even too cheap. Then offer your option and move forward with certainty that the person has accepted it.

For example, say Staples wants to promote a certain printer in their color circular coming out this weekend. They can have an image of a more expensive printer on the left. They center and enlarge the picture of the printer they want to promote, and then they have a third, inferior and cheaper option on the right. This strategy is proven to increase sales.

8. Solve Obstacles That Exist . . .

. . . in advance.

Most persuaders try to think of comebacks. You should have long ago thought about every possible path the communication could have taken. Solve all possible obstacles in advance. Then, at the time of the interaction, do not solve them too quickly, or you make the client feel foolish or stupid.

Always expect objections that will slow down the process. They are normal. You should be highlighting the weaknesses in your product as you go along, so that you have long ago addressed any objections.

Don't your current customers present similar objections? "I don't have the money" and so on? Figure out your answer beforehand and know how you will answer. For example, "That's exactly why you need to pick up this product today. This product may just be exactly what you need to illuminate this issue for you."

9. Ask Until They Say Yes

If the person should say yes to you, then make sure you cause them to say yes. If they should say no to you, then make darned sure they say no.

Develop your skill of persistence. Know when your proposal is right for your customer and persist until they say yes, knowing full well it's sometimes important that they say no.

10. Validate Later

Know that after they have said yes, they will experience near instant regret for a few days. This is true whether the woman is picking one man over another or choosing one car over another. You must validate the person's decision. Not immediately after the consummation of the deal, but a day later.

People have been conditioned to regret their past purchases. Their mistakes of the past have been imprinted on their mind. (This is a problem you need to presolve, as well.)

My friend, Katherin, commented on a new sweater she had bought. I told her it was nice and asked, "Was it expensive?" She said, "Yessss." When I asked her how expensive, she replied, "Well, when you figure the cost per use. . . ." She had solved her own feeling of regret and validated her own purchase!

"Isn't it worth the price of a cup of coffee for you to have this . . ."

Option Attachment comes into play upon making a decision. Be aware that this commonly occurs and have a means to defuse it.

A congratulations note a few days after the purchase of a product or service can go a long way toward eliminating regret.

Bibliography

Anseel, F., and W. Duyck. 2008. "Unconscious Applicants: A Systematic Test of the Name-Letter Effect." *Psychological Science* 9(10): 1059–1061.

Aronson, E. 1995. *The Social Animal*. New York, NY: W. H. Freeman and Company.

Association for Psychological Science. 2007. "What's in a Name? Initials Linked to Success, Study Shows." Press release, November 14.

Baumeister, R. F., and J. Tierney. 2011. *Willpower: Rediscovering the Greatest Human Strength*. New York, NY: Penguin Books.

Belsky, G., and T. Gilovich. 1999. *Why Smart People Make Big Money Mistakes and How to Correct Them*. New York, NY: Fireside.

Bertrand, M., D. Karlan, S. Mullainathan, E. Shafir, and J. Zinman. 2010. February. "What's Advertising Content Worth? Evidence From a Consumer Credit Marketing Field Experiment." *The Quarterly Journal of Economics* (February): 263–306.

Bethel, W. 1995. *10 Steps to Connecting With Your Customer: Communication Skills for Selling Your Products, Services, and Ideas*. Chicago, IL: The Dartnell Corporation.

Bloom, H. 1995. *The Lucifer Principle: A Scientific Expedition into the Forces of History*. New York, NY: Atlantic Monthly Press.

Brodie, R. 1996. *Virus of the Mind: The New Science of the Meme*. Seattle, WA: Integral Press.

Burger, J. M., N. Messian, S. Patel, A. del Prado, and C. Anderson. 2004, January. "What a Coincidence! The Effects of Incidental Similarity on Compliance." *Personality and Social Psychology Bulletin* 30(1): 35–43.

Burger, J. M., S. Soroka, K. Gonzago, E. Murphy, and E. Somervel. 2001. "The Effect of Fleeting Attraction on Compliance to Requests." *Personality and Social Psychology Bulletin* 27(12): 1578–1586.

Carlson, K. A., and J. M. Conard. 2011, January. "The Last Name Effect: How Last Name Influences Acquisition Timing." *Journal of Consumer Research* 38(2).

Cialdini, R. B. 1993. *Influence: Science and Practice.* New York, NY: Morrow.

Cohen, A. R., and D. L. Bradford. 1991. *Influence without Authority.* New York, NY: John Wiley & Sons.

Crano, William D. 2012 *The Rules of Influence: Winning when You're in the Minority.* New York, NY: St. Martin's Press.

Dalet, K., and E. Wolfe. 1996. *Socratic Selling: How to Ask the Questions that Get the Sale.* Chicago, IL: Irwin Professional Publishing.

Dayton, D. 1997. *Selling Microsoft, Sales Secrets from Inside the World's Most Successful Company.* Holbrook, MA: Dayton.

Dillard, J., and M. Pfau. 2004. *The Persuasion Handbook: Developments in Theory and Practice.* Thousand Oaks, CA: Sage Publications.

Dawson, R. 1992. *Secrets of Power Persuasion: Everything You'll Ever Need to Get Anything You'll Ever Want.* Englewood Cliffs, NJ: Prentice-Hall.

Dolinski, D., and K. Szczucka. 2008. "Seesaw of Emotions and Compliance." *Journal of Experimental Social Psychology* 34:27–50.

Eagleman, D. 2011. *Incognito: The Secret Lives of the Brain.* New York, NY: Vintage Books.

Eden, D., and A. Shani. 1982, April. "Pygmalion Goes to Boot Camp: Expectancy, Leadership, and Trainee Performance." *Journal of Applied Psychology* 67(2): 194–199.

Farber, B. J., and J. Wycoff. 1992. *Breakthrough Selling: Customer-Building Strategies from the Best in the Business.* Englewood Cliffs, NJ: Prentice-Hall.

Forgas, J. P., and K. D. Williams. 2001. *Social Influence: Direct and Indirect Processes.* Philadelphia, PA: Psychology Press.

Garner, R. 2005. "Post-It Note Persuasion: A Sticky Influence." *Journal of Consumer Psychology.*

Gass, R., and J. Seiter. 2004. *Persuasion, Social Influence and Compliance Gaining.* New York, NY: Allyn & Bacon.

Gilovich, T., D. Griffin, and D. Kahneman. 2004. *Heuristics and Biases: The Psychology of Intuitive Judgment.* New York, NY: University of Cambridge Press.

Gitomer, J. 1994. *The Sales Bible: The Ultimate Sales Resource.* New York, NY: William Morrow.

Gregory, W. L., R. B. Cialdini, and K. M. Carpenter. 1982. "Self-Relevant Scenarios as Mediators of Likelihood Estimates and Compliance: Does Imaging Make It So?" *Journal of Personality and Social Psychology* 43: 89–99.

Hamer, D. 1998. *Living With Our Genes: Why They Matter More Than You Think.* New York, NY: Doubleday.

Hogan, K. 1996. *The Psychology of Persuasion: How to Persuade Others to Your Way of Thinking.* Gretna, LA: Pelican.

Hogan, K. 2000. *Through the Open Door: Secrets of Self Hypnosis.* Gretna, LA: Pelican.

Hogan, K. 2001. *Irresistible Attraction: Secrets of Personal Magnetism.* Eagan, MN: Network 3000 Publishing.

Hogan, K. 2004. *Science of Influence* Eagan, MN: Network 3000 Publishing.

Itti, L., and P. Baldi. 2005. "Bayesian Surprise Attracts Human Attention." *Neural Information Processing Systems* 19: 547–554.

Johnson, K. L. 1994. *Sales Magic: Revolutionary New Techniques That Will Double Your Sales Volume in 21 Days.* New York, NY: William Morrow.

Johnson, K. L. 1988. *Subliminal Selling Skills.* New York, NY: AMACOM.

Kahneman, D., and A. Tversky. 2000. *Choices, Values and Frames.* New York, NY: Russell Sage Foundation.

Kalist, D. E., and D. Y. Lee. 2009, January. "First Names and Crime: Does Unpopularity Spell Trouble?" *Social Science Quarterly* 90: 39–49.

Kennedy, D. S. 1990. *The Ultimate Sales Letter.* Holbrook, MA: Bob Adams.

Kenrick, D. 2011. *Sex, Murder, and the Meaning of Life: A Psychologist Investigates How Evolution, Cognition, and Complexity are Revolutionizing Our View of Human Nature.* New York, NY: Basic Books.

Kent, R. W. 1963. *The Art of Persuasion.* Surfside, FL: Lee Institute.

Kettle, K. L., and G. Häubl. 2011, October. "The Signature Effect: Signing Influence Consumption-Related Behavior by Priming Self-Identity." *Journal of Consumer Research* 38: 474–489.

Knapp, M., and J. Hall. 1992. *Nonverbal Communication in Human Interaction,* 3rd ed. Fort Worth, TX: Harcourt Brace College Publications.

Knight, S. 1995. *NLP at Work: The Difference That Makes A Difference in Business.* Sonoma, CA: Nicholas Brealey.

Knowles, E. S., and J. A. Linn. 2003. *Resistance and Persuasion.* Mahwah, NJ: Lawrence Erlbaum Associates.

Kostere, K. 1989. *Get the Results You Want: A Systematic Approach to NLP.* Portland, OR: Metamorphous Press.

Lavington, C., and S. Losee. 1997. *You've Only Got Three Seconds: How to Make the Right Impression in your Business and Social Life.* New York, NY: Doubleday.

Lewis, D. 1990. *The Secret Language of Success: Using Body Language to Get What You Want.* New York, NY: Carroll & Graf.

Linden, A., and K. Perutz. 1997. *Mindworks: Unlock the Promise Within— NLP Tools for Building a Better Life.* Kansas City, MO: Andrews McMeel Publishing.

Loftus, E. and J. Palmer. 1974. "Reconstruction of Automobile Destruction: An Example of the Interaction Between Language and Memory". *Journal of Verbal Learning and Verbal Behavior,* 13, 585–589.

Mehrabian, A. 1981. *Silent Messages: Implicit Communication of Emotions and Attitudes.* Belmont, CA: Wadsworth.

Miller, G. 2010. *Spent: Sex, Evolution, and Consumer Behavior.* New York, NY: Viking.

Moine, D. J., and J. H. Herd. 1984. *Modern Persuasion Strategies: The Hidden Advantage in Selling.* Englewood Cliffs, NJ: Prentice-Hall.

Moine, D. J., and K. Lloyd. 1990. *Unlimited Selling Power: How to Master Hypnotic Selling Skills.* Englewood Cliffs, NJ: Prentice-Hall.

Myers, D. G. 2003. *Intuition: Its Powers and Perils.* New Haven, CT: Yale University Press.

Narwat, R., and D. Dolinski. 1998, January). "'Fear-Then-Relief' Procedure for Producing Compliance: Beware When the Danger Is Over." *Journal of Experimental Social Psychology* 34(1), 27–50.

Nelson, L., and J. Simmons. 2007, November 14. "Moniker Maladies: When Names Sabotage Success." *Psychological Science* 14: 106–110.

O'Keefe, D. J. 2003. *Persuasion: Theory and Research.* Thousand Oaks, CA: Sage Publications.

Overstreet, H. A. 1925. *Influencing Human Behavior.* New York, NY: Norton.

Park, J. K., and John, D. R. 2010, December. "Got to Get You into My Life: Do Brand Personalities Rub Off on Consumers?" *Journal of Consumer Research* 37(4): 655–669.

Patton, F. H. 1986. *Force of Persuasion: Dynamic Techniques for Influencing People.* Englewood Cliffs, NJ: Prentice-Hall.

Pelham, B. W., M. C. Mirenberg, and J. T. Jones. 2002. "Why Susie Sells Seashells by the Seashore: Implicit Egotism and Major Life Decisions." *Journal of Personality and Social Psychology* 82(4): 469–487.

Perloff, R. 1993. *The Dynamics of Persuasion.* Hillside, NJ: Lawrence Erlbaum Associates.

Piirto, R. 1991. *Beyond Mind Games: The Marketing Power of Psychographics.* Ithaca, NY: American Demographic Books.

Peoples, D. 1993. *Selling to the Top.* New York, NY: John Wiley & Sons.

Plous, S. 1993. *The Psychology of Judgment and Decision Making.* New York, NY: McGraw-Hill.

Qubein, N. 1983. *Professional Selling Techniques: Strategies and Tactics to Boost Your Selling Skills and Build Your Career.* Rockville Centre, NY: Farnsworth Publishing Co..

Richardson, J. 1988. *The Magic of Rapport.* Capitola, CA: Meta Publications.

Robbins, A. 1987. *Unlimited Power.* New York, NY: Fawcett.

Robertson, J. E. 1990. *Sales: The Mind's Side—What They Didn't Teach You in Sales Training.* Portland, OR: Metamorphous Press.

Sadovsky, M. C., and J. Caswell. 1996. *Selling the Way Your Customer Buys: Understand Your Prospects' Unspoken Needs & Close Every Sale.* New York, NY: AMACOM.

Sherman, S. J., M. T. Crawford, and A. R. McConnell. 2004. "Looking Ahead as a Technique to Reduce Resistance to Persuasive Attempts." In *Resistance and Persuasion,* edited by E. S. Knowles and J. A. Linn (149–174). Mahwah, NJ: Lawrence Erlbaum Associates.

Snyder, M., E. Tanke, and E. Berscheid. 1977, September. "Social Perception and Interpersonal Behavior: On the Self-Fulfilling Nature of Social Stereotypes." *Journal of Personality and Social Psychology* 35(9): 656–666.

Sutherland, S. 1992. *Irrationality: Why We Don't Think Straight.* New Brunswick, NJ: Rutgers University Press.

Thaler, R. 1992. *The Winner's Curse: Paradoxes and Anomalies of Economic Life.* Princeton, NJ: Princeton University Press.

Thompson, G. J., and J. B. Jenkins. 1993. *Verbal Judo: The Gentle Art of Persuasion.* New York, NY: William Morrow.

Wansink, B. 2006. *Mindless Eating: Why We Eat More Than We Think.* New York, NY: Bantam Dell.

Wegner, D. 2002. *The Illusion of Conscious Will.* Cambridge, MA: Bradford Books, MIT Press.

Willingham, R. 1984. *The Best Seller: The New Psychology of Selling and Persuading People.* Englewood Cliffs, NJ: Prentice-Hall.

Wilson, T. D. 2002. *Strangers to Ourselves: Discovering the Adaptive Unconscious.* Cambridge, MA: Belknap Press of Harvard University.

Witte, K., and M. Allen. 2000. "A Meta-Analysis of Fear Appeals: Implications for Effective Public Health Campaigns." *Health, Education and Behavior* 27: 291–615.

Zimbardo, P. G. 1991. *The Psychology of Attitude Change and Social Influence.* New York, NY: McGraw-Hill.

Index

About the Author

Kevin Hogan could be an excellent choice for your next event. His fast-paced style is entertaining and information packed. Keynotes, three-hour, and full-day presentations are available.

You can reach Kevin at kevin@kevinhogan.com.

To see Kevin on video, visit www.kevinhogan.net.

To check out his biography, go to www.kevinhogan.com/biography .htm.

If you'd like a free copy of his e-book, *Mind Access,* and a no-cost subscription to *Coffee with Kevin Hogan,* go to www.kevinhogan.com and drop in your name and email address—you'll get both immediately.